ALL
CHILDISH
THINGS

All Childish Things

ISBN-13: 978-1944540166
ISBN-10: 1944540164

For information about production rights, visit:
www.jzettelmaier.com

Published by Sordelet Ink
Cover by David Blixt

ALL CHILDISH THINGS

A PLAY BY

JOSEPH ZETTELMAIER

Published by
Sordelet Ink

ALL CHILDISH THINGS premiered at the Planet Ant Theatre, in Hamtramck, Michigan on June 23, 2006. It was directed by Eric Maher, and produced by Jaime Moyer. Set design by Eric Maher. Lighting design by Curtis Green. Costume design by Joe Colosi. Stage managed by Curtis Green. Assistant directed by Shannon Ferrante. The cast was as follows:

DAVE BULLANSKI: Peter C. Prouty
MAX FARLEY: Joe Colosi
CARTER SLOAN: Chris Roady
KENDRA JOHNSON: Kelly Rossi
THE BIG MAN: Joel Mitchell

ALL CHILDISH THINGS received its Equity premiere at the BoarsHead Theatre in Lansing, Michigan on October 24, 2008. It was directed by Joey Albright. Set and lighting design by Daniel C. Walker. Costume design by Holly Iler. Sound design by Sergei Kvitko. Props design by Patricia York. Stage managed by Katie Doyle. The cast was as follows:

DAVE BULLANSKI: Jason Richards
MAX FARLEY: Aral B. Gribble III
CARTER SLOAN: Brian D. Thibault
KENDRA JOHNSON: Molly Thomas
THE BIG MAN: Keith Allan Kalinowski

ALL CHILDISH THINGS WAS A NOMINEE FOR THE 2006 AMERICAN THEATRE CRITICS ASSOCIATION/STEINBERG NEW PLAY AWARD.

Cast of Characters

DAVE BULLANSKI, computer programmer, 30s
MAX FARLEY, mover, 30s
CARTER SLOAN, stock boy with Kenner Toys, 30s
KENDRA JOHNSON, movie theatre employee, 20s
The BIG MAN, 40s

Time

2006

Place

Cincinnati, near the warehouses
for Kenner Toys

ACT I

(Lights up. DAVE's basement. It is set up with Star Wars regalia over every inch of the place. In a corner with its back facing the audience sits a huge cabinet. As lights rise, DAVE enters. He carries a bag of groceries. He goes around the room, checking everything. He's clearly stressed out, trying to calm down as he works. He grabs a Star Wars stress ball while looking through CDs. He picks one and listens to it while he lights up a cigarette. His cellphone rings)

DAVE
What? Whatwhatwhat? *(listens)*
No, mom. It's fine. The doors are locked. *(listens)*
Yep, he got his food. Hold on. *(listens)*
(He turns down the music)
Sorry, I couldn't... *(listens)*
Spencer's fine. *(listens)*
I don't know. Probably under the couch, being fat. *(listens)*

He's not our cat. He's your... *(listens)*
Mom.
Mom.
MOM!
I can love you and not love him. You're not a package deal. *(listens)*
Just...look, just enjoy Vegas, ok? Everything is secure. *(listens)*
I won't let the place burn down. I live here too.
Ok.
Ok.
Goodbye.
Mom.
Goodbye.
Mom.
Mom.
Mom.
Goodbye.
Mom.
MOM!
GOODBYE!

(He hangs up the phone. He grabs his stress ball and begins to squeeze it frantically. As he paces, he smells something odd. He walks the room, trying to determine the origin. He sees some files he's left on the coffee table. He picks one up, smells it, recoils)

DAVE
Dammit, Spencer! Where are you? *(He looks under a few things)* You can't hide forever, you furry bastard. *(He stands up, trying to calm himself)* Alright, dude. Keep it together. You're flipping out. Now is not the time to be flipping out. Just calm down.

(He goes over to the cabinet, and is about to open it. Suddenly, a knock on the basement window. DAVE jumps)

DAVE
Jeez!

(He turns to see MAX at the window, waving)

DAVE
(Yelling to MAX) Come around the front. I'll let you in. *(DAVE exits. Offstage, we hear MAX & DAVE talk as they return)*

MAX
Hey, dude.

DAVE
Hey. What'd you get?

MAX
Meat lovers.

DAVE
You do realize that Kendra's a vegetarian, right?

MAX
I do. I do realize that.

(DAVE laughs. They appear at the stairway, and enter the basement)

MAX
So they're not here?

DAVE
Not yet.

MAX
Wait. Really?

DAVE
Yeah.

MAX
But...but I thought we were supposed to meet at
10:00. It's like fifteen til. What if...

DAVE
They'll be here, dude.

MAX
But...but...

DAVE
They'll. Be. Here.

*(MAX sets down the pizza and takes a slice. DAVE
gets a Mountain Dew out of the mini-fridge)*

MAX
Somethin' smells like cat pee.

DAVE
Spencer peed on the files.

MAX
Oh. *(Beat)* We have files?

DAVE
Yep.

MAX
Why?

DAVE
Because if we're going to get this done right, it's
going to require split-second timing and compre-
hensive information. I've mapped out everything
we'll need and put it into packets.

(Beat. MAX stares at the packets, concerned)

DAVE
What?

MAX
Bad feeling.

DAVE
Max, don't...

MAX
Your cat...

DAVE
Mom's cat.

MAX
...pees on the files. Not a good sign.

DAVE
He's an asshole. He pees on everything.

MAX
You gotta figure though...there's a lot of places to pee in here. If he jumped up on that table, and peed on those files...it's because he chose to.

DAVE
Don't make this into...

MAX
Bad feeling, man. Bad. Feeling.

(They stare at the files. Beat. DAVE grabs his Mountain Dew)

DAVE
Oh yeah. There we go.

MAX
Don't...don't you think maybe you've had enough?

(DAVE glares at him)

MAX
Know what? I just...you're good.

(MAX paces, trying to work off nervous energy. MAX grabs a Mountain Dew. DAVE starts psyching himself up, energy rising)

DAVE
So tonight's the night. You ready?

MAX
Yes. I think so. Yes. Maybe. Are you ready?

DAVE
Oh, I'm ready.

MAX
We can do this, right? Tell me we can do this.

DAVE
Oh yeah. This is gonna go off without a hitch.

MAX
How do you know?

DAVE
Five months of planning. That's how I know. When it's all over...we're gonna be wealthy, wealthy men.

MAX
And one woman.

DAVE
Ugh. Fine. *(Raises his Mountain Dew to MAX)* To five hundred thousand.

(Beat)

MAX
I thought it was 2 million.

DAVE
Divided four ways is five hundred thousand.

MAX
Oh. Right. (Clinks his drink with DAVE's) I'm gonna buy a house. Yep. That's what I'm gonna do.

DAVE
I was thinking the same thing. I've gotta get out of this basement.

MAX
And...and....I'm gonna invest the rest. Yeah. I'm gonna get one of those guys who're good with money...

DAVE
A broker.

MAX
Yeah. And I'm gonna make my money make more money. And I'm gonna retire at 45, and I'm gonna be a millionaire and it'll be sweet. What're you gonna do with your share?

DAVE
Oh, I've got plans.

MAX
Yeah?

DAVE
Big plans.

MAX
Like what?

DAVE
Don't you worry about that, my friend.

MAX
Gotta worry about something.

DAVE
No, you don't. We're all good.

MAX
(Pacing the room) Maybe tonight was band prac-
tice. Maybe Carter's there and we're just...

DAVE
Dude. We were talking about this two days ago.
He's just running late.

MAX
Maybe Funk Force has a show tonight and...

DAVE
Do you want me to call him? Will that make you
feel better?

MAX
Yes please.

(DAVE grabs his phone, dials)

DAVE
Hey, man. Gimme an ETA.
Oh, Max is freaking out.

MAX
I'm not...shut up!

DAVE
I know, right? Huge surprise.

MAX
Carter! I'm not freaking out!

(DAVE puts a finger up to silence him)

DAVE
Cool. Thanks, man.
No, you rock!
(Hangs up)
He's almost here.

MAX
Why'd you tell him I was freaking out?

DAVE
...because you were freaking out?

(MAX paces nervously)

DAVE
Sit down.

MAX
I can't. I'm nervous.

DAVE
Why?

MAX
He peed on the files, man! He peed! On the files!

DAVE
That doesn't mean anything!

MAX
What if you're wrong? What if this turns into one huge cluster-fuck?! I mean, shit, dude. I've never done anything illegal in my whole life. I mean, not real illegal. I can't go to jail, you understand me? Who's gonna provide for Carrie? I mean... fuck!

(Beat)

MAX
I'm out. That's it. I'm out.

DAVE
You're not out.

MAX
Enjoy the pizza, and try not to get busted.

DAVE
Max. Look at me. Look. At. Me.

(MAX meets DAVE's eyes)

DAVE
Me, you, Carter. How long have we known each
other?

MAX
A long time.

DAVE
How long?

MAX
Since we were five.

DAVE
Since we were...exactly. A long time ago, on one
magical Halloween. You remember?

MAX
(Smiles) Yeah, maybe.

DAVE
Well, let me refresh your memory. A little boy
in a Darth Vader costume is walking back home,
his bag full of candy. A group of fourth-graders come riding up on their ten-speeds, swing-
ing socks full of soap. The little boy runs, turns
to sidewalks and back alleys, but he can't lose the

enemy. Suddenly, the little boy is trapped behind Mr. Farley's shed. The fourth-graders closing in, their eyes full of blood and candy-lust. And then, from the darkness, a shadowy figure leaps out of a tree, landing flat on the fourth-grader leader. A glorious battle ensues, and when the dust clears, those little bastards are running home to their momma's! Now tell me, Max, who was that little boy in the Darth Vader costume!?

MAX
You were.

DAVE
And who was that brave kid who came to my rescue?

MAX
I was.

DAVE
Who was?!

MAX
I WAS!

DAVE
You're damn right you were! Because you're Max Farley, goddammit! You are without fear! You are Chewbacca, and I wanna hear your battle cry.

(MAX wants to, but is a little shy)

DAVE
Come on, Chewie! Let me hear your battle cry.

(MAX roars quietly)

DAVE
Louder, you wild Wookie! Scream to the heavens!

(MAX roars loudly, proudly)

DAVE
Now that's the Max Farley I know. The bravest son of a bitch to ever come out of Carson Elementary.

MAX
Yeah!

DAVE
Now listen to me when I say these words-I will never let anything happen to you. Never.

(They stare at each other for a moment. Then MAX grabs DAVE in a bear hug)

MAX
I love you, buddy.

DAVE
I love you too, man.

(They let each other go)

DAVE
All right. I have to hit the bathroom. Now...

(DAVE retrieves a lightsaber from the shelf)

DAVE
I figured Carter might be late, so I pulled out my lightsaber. You can play with it if you want.

MAX
Is it the blue one?

DAVE
It's the blue one.

MAX
That's my favorite.

DAVE
I know.

MAX
Thanks, man.

DAVE
No problem. *(Goes to the bathroom)*

(MAX sits down. He plays for a little while, but his eyes keep drifting to the cabinet. He soon finds himself standing in front of it. Almost against his will, he finds his hands undoing the first of many locks. Suddenly, an alarm goes off)

DAVE
(Running out of the bathroom) What are you doing?!

MAX
I'm sorry!

DAVE
You tried to open the cabinet.

MAX
I didn't mean to! I just...it was like I couldn't control myself.

DAVE
Yes. The cabinet can have a powerful effect on the weak-minded. *(Goes to the cabinet, losing himself in his own thoughts. He touches the cabinet)* I have to be careful, man. This is my life's work...my Mona Lisa. My 8th symphony.

MAX
I know. I'm sorry.

DAVE
Every figure, mint in box. Every special offer.

Every import I could get through customs. Each individual piece becoming part of something greater, something...

MAX
Magnificent.

(DAVE looks to him, nods)

DAVE
Magnificent.

MAX
I just...if I could just look at it again, maybe get a spritz of the Eau Lando cologne...

DAVE
Carter wants to show it to Kendra. When they get here, we can all look. For eighteen seconds.

MAX
OK.

DAVE
You realize that you and Carter are the only people who've seen this? That is how much I trust you.

MAX
What about your mom?

DAVE
Please. She'd take one look at them and they'd be in a garage sale next week.

(Beat)

MAX
Man, that's not funny.

DAVE
Right? I've had reoccurring nightmares about that.

(MAX goes to the window)

DAVE
They'll get here, Max.

MAX
When?

DAVE
Soon.

MAX
They're late.

DAVE
They're always late. Kendra probably had to make sure she brought enough bitch for everyone.

MAX
Man, you never stop, do you?

DAVE
Everyone needs a hobby.

MAX
Well, you better start gettin' used to her.

(Beat)

DAVE
What exactly does that mean?

MAX
I think she's the one. For him. Not for me. Obviously.

DAVE
Excuse me?

MAX
I think they're gonna end up getting hitched.

(DAVE just stares at him)

MAX
Oh, come on. The thought's never occurred to you?

DAVE
No, it hasn't.

MAX
They've been together a while, man. And he still likes her.

DAVE
I'm sure he's got someone on the side.

MAX
Nope.

DAVE
It's Carter. He's got someone.

MAX
Nope.

DAVE
How do you know?

MAX
He told me.

DAVE
That doesn't mean anything.

MAX
If he was foolin' around, we'd know. He'd be over here bragging about it right now. But he's not. He's with her.

(DAVE says nothing)

MAX
Remember New Years? He bought them those tickets on the Delta Queen? They sailed down the river and did all that romantic stuff.

DAVE
He just wanted to play Blackjack. She tagged along.

MAX
No way, dude. That was a looooooove cruise. It wasn't about the gambling. It was about the looooooooove.

(DAVE, frustrated, tosses a black ski mask at MAX)

MAX
What's this?

DAVE
Your mask. For tonight.

MAX
This isn't my mask.

DAVE
Yes it is.

MAX
You said I'd have a Chewbacca mask!

DAVE
Oh my god. That was like 3 months ago.

MAX
I was supposed to be Chewbacca, you were gonna be Luke, Carter was gonna be Han, and Kendra was gonna be Leia. That was the plan.

DAVE
We're not going to be running around in Star Wars masks. It's too conspicuous.

MAX
I can't believe you're changing the plan.

DAVE
I don't have time to go over everything in committee, Max.

MAX
I am not a committee!

DAVE
Oh my god, you're killing me...

MAX
You're changing shit on me last minute. I do not handle change well, Dave. You know this. I have high blood pressure.

DAVE
It's just a mask.

MAX
I got my physical; know what the doctor said to me? I'm "high-risk". Said I need to drop like thirty pounds. And...now this is the important thing, Dave...he said I should try and avoid unnecessary stress.

DAVE
An even split of 2 million dollars is pretty freaking necessary.

MAX
See, you can say that 'cause you don't have as much to lose. I've got a kid, man! None of you guys get it. The biggest thing in your life is that cabinet.

And what's Carter got to lose? His bimbo-of-the-week?

DAVE
But what about the looooove?

MAX
That's not the point! The thing is...you guys can make these big plans 'cause no one depends on you. But...Carrie's four, man. She needs me.

DAVE
And with the money you're getting tonight, you can really give her the kind of life she deserves, that you both deserve.

MAX
Just...no more surprises, ok?

DAVE
OK.

(Suddenly, a timer sounds on DAVE's desk. MAX jumps, and DAVE runs to the computer)

MAX
OH GOD! What the fuck!?

DAVE
Dude, online auction. Chill out. (Types furiously on the computer) Ha! Take that, pronerd72@gmail. com!

MAX
What'd you win?

DAVE
A still-sealed package of 1977 Star Wars Dixie cups.

MAX
Still sealed?

DAVE
Oh yeah. That's right.

MAX
Nice. How much?

DAVE
(Shrugs, types on the computer for a bit) That's what I'm looking forward to.

MAX
Dixie Cups?

DAVE
Not having to worry about "how much".

MAX
That what you're gonna use the money for? To feed your habit?

DAVE
Some of it, sure. And don't call it a habit. I'm a collector, not a junkie.

MAX
Fine line, my friend. Very fine line.

DAVE
Please, if you had my job and my lack of real responsibilities, you'd be the same way.

(Dave's phone rings. MAX grabs it first)

MAX
It's your mom.

DAVE
Ugh. Let it go to voicemail.

MAX
Dude. Weak. It's your mom.

DAVE
No, wait! Don't...

(MAX answers)

MAX
Hey, Mrs. B.
No, it's Max.
Dave's...in the bathroom. He's pooping.

DAVE
Jesus...

MAX
We're just hanging out.
No, just the four of us tonight.

DAVE
(An angry whisper) Shut up!

(MAX waves him off, mouths "I got this.")

MAX
Me, Dave, Carter, and Kendra.
You remember Kendra.
Carter's girlfriend.
I know, right?! Like over a year now.
Believe me, if I knew a nice girl for Dave, I'd keep
her for myself.
No, I got divorced.
Yeah.
2 years ago.
Mm-hmm.
Mm-hmm.
Yeah, no, it was super depressing.

(Beat. MAX is now saddened & regretting having picked up the phone)

MAX
So I'm gonna go now.
I'll remind him about Spencer's meds.
Ok bye now.

(He hangs up, tosses the phone to DAVE)

DAVE
That's why you let it go to voicemail.

(MAX sits. DAVE goes to him)

DAVE
She doesn't mean to go for the jugular. It just kind of happens.

(DAVE goes to the groceries, hands a box of Ding-Dongs to MAX, who immediately brightens)

MAX
Hey! Ding-Dongs.

(The doorbell rings)

DAVE
God! Finally! *(He shouts up the stairs)* I'm coming, Carter. Just...

(Pounding on the door)

CARTER
(Offstage) Mr. Bullanski? This is Detective Harrison with the Norwood PD. Mr. Bullanski?

(MAX begins to panic, loudly whispering to DAVE)

MAX
Oh shit! DUDE! Shit! Dude! Dude! Shit, dude!

DAVE
What?!

CARTER
(*Offstage*) Mr. Bullanski, please open the door. I won't ask again.

MAX
We gotta get out of here! Is there like a window or...?! (*He runs around, trying to find a way out*)

CARTER
(*Offstage*) We're coming in, Mr. Bullanski. No funny business!

DAVE
Wait!

MAX
Oh god, I'm sorry!

(*CARTER starts to yell as he and KENDRA run down the stairs, into the basement. He is wearing his band's t-shirt. He stares at them smiling, while they stare at him unmoving. He points his forefingers at them, making laser-gun sounds*)

CARTER
Pyew pyew, pyew pyew pyew.

(*Beat. MAX & DAVE say nothing KENDRA is trying hard not to laugh. The following dialog is rapid-fire*)

CARTER
Get it? Like in the Death Star? And he saw the stormtroopers and ran back...

DAVE
You asshole!

MAX
Oh man...oh my freakin' heart...

DAVE
Why?! Why would you do that?!

CARTER
Because it was hilarious?

KENDRA
It kinda was.

DAVE
Don't you start!

MAX
Ok...just gotta breathe...

KENDRA
What smells like cat pee?

DAVE
Do you get what we're doing tonight?

MAX
Spencer peed on the files.

CARTER
It was a joke!

KENDRA
We have files?

DAVE
This shit is serious!

MAX
We've had them for months, Kendra. Try to keep up, OK?

CARTER
OK. I'm sorry. Really.

KENDRA
Hey, don't talk to me like that, wide-load.

DAVE
Sorry?

KENDRA
Carter!

DAVE
Sorry?!

KENDRA
Carter!

DAVE
Sorry is for screw-ups and Alderaan!

MAX
What'd you call me?

KENDRA
Are you gonna let him talk to me like that?

CARTER
Honey, just...

MAX
Are you gonna let her talk to me like that?

CARTER
Guys, seriously, indoor voices.

DAVE
Why the hell is she even here? She's just pissing
everyone off.

KENDRA
I am not!

CARTER
Please. My head...

DAVE
Look! You're giving him a headache. Happy?

(CARTER pulls a gun out of his jacket. Everyone freezes)

DAVE
Whoa. Whoa. Just calm down. You don't have to shoot anyone, OK? Except maybe her.

(CARTER puts the gun away)

CARTER
I'm not gonna shoot anyone. I just...I need you guys to be quiet. This is stressful enough without you three falling apart on me. So please...I love all of you...but you have got to just shut up. OK?

MAX
Yes. I'm sorry.

DAVE
OK.

KENDRA
Sure.

(Beat)

MAX
So...you've got a gun.

CARTER
Yes, I do.

MAX
Um. Why?

CARTER
Because sometimes shit happens.

MAX
Ok, see! That's what I'm talking about! That's why I'm gonna have a heart attack.

DAVE
(to CARTER) Max is having some stress management issues.

KENDRA
He should try dropping 80 pounds.

MAX
Hey!

(Beat)

MAX
Shut up. And it's 30 pounds.

CARTER
Dave, open the cabinet.

DAVE
What?

CARTER
Everyone's freaking out. It'll put things in perspective. Open the cabinet.

DAVE
Yeah. Yeah, OK.

(DAVE opens the cabinet. They all huddle around its luminescence)

CARTER
See, look at that. It just...I don't know...

MAX
It makes the world a better place.

CARTER
Yeah, man. Exactly.

(All stare in awe, except KENDRA, who clearly couldn't care less)

CARTER
C'mon, baby. That's awesome and you know it.

KENDRA
Sure.

CARTER
You can't look at that and tell me it's not awesome.

(KENDRA stares at the cabinet, then looks CARTER dead in the eyes)

KENDRA
It's not awesome.

(DAVE slams it shut, and speaks to CARTER, refusing to acknowledge KENDRA)

DAVE
That's it. She's out.

CARTER
She's not out.

KENDRA
Yeah!

DAVE
I will not let this soulless nerf-herder bring the whole operation down!

KENDRA
Nerf-herder? What the hell is that?

MAX
"Scruffy looking nerf-herder." Hello? Empire Strikes Back.

KENDRA
God! Can you guys talk anything other than Star Trek?

(MAX & DAVE stare at KENDRA in shock. Even CARTER is surprised by her Sci-Fi faux pas)

MAX
Wow.

DAVE
I...I don't even know what to say to this.

KENDRA
What?

DAVE
Carter, it's talking to me. Tell it to stop talking to me.

CARTER
Am I gonna have to pull out the gun again? Huh? Am I?

(Beat)

DAVE
Sorry, Carter,

MAX
I'll be good.

CARTER
Ok, by my watch...

(CARTER checks his watch)

CARTER
...we gotta head outta here in 20 minutes. First things first-Dave. What smells like cat pee?

DAVE
Just...dammit, gimme a second.

(DAVE grabs the files and exits upstairs. An awkward silence hangs between them)

MAX
So...um...Funk Force t-shirt.

CARTER
Pretty badass, right?

KENDRA
Seriously, the new merchandise is soooo cool.

CARTER
Thanks, baby.

(They kiss)

MAX
Right, but...

CARTER
The key was getting the whole band front-and-center. Bass players always get screwed. I told Jimmy "no more background shit, man."

KENDRA
Right? You started the band, you should be the face!

CARTER
This is why I love her.

MAX
Ok, but my concern is...

CARTER
I know, dude. They weren't cheap. But come on. Funk Force!

KENDRA
I'm actually shooting their first video next month. We're going into the subway tunnels and...

MAX
Carter! Do you really wanna commit a major crime wearing your band's t-shirt?!

(CARTER smiles, pats a duffel bag he came in with)

CARTER
No worries. I got it covered.

(KENDRA glares at MAX)

KENDRA
You never believed in Funk Force.

(MAX glares at KENDRA)

MAX
Pizza?

(KENDRA stares at it)

KENDRA
Wow. That sure is a lot of dead animal.

MAX
Delicious dead animal.

KENDRA
Do you know how many species are now extinct because...?

(CARTER takes a piece)

MAX
This is gonna work, isn't it, Carter?

CARTER
Like busting Han outta Jabba's palace.

KENDRA
Don't get started.

MAX
Hey. He's cheering me up.

KENDRA
I can't figure out how you guys have been friends for 20 years with nothing else to talk about.

MAX
That's 'cause...you don't even...shut up.

KENDRA
Seriously. There's more to life than those freaking movies.

CARTER
Hon, c'mon.

KENDRA
No! You always take their side, but I have a valid point here. Let's say, hypothetically, Star Wars never existed.

(MAX is about to say something)

KENDRA
I mean all of them. No Empire Strikes Back, no Jedi, no...what's the real name for the first one?

CARTER & MAX
A New Hope.

KENDRA
Right. Say none of them existed...

MAX
No. I won't say that.

KENDRA
What would you guys talk about? Sports? Politics? What? Give me something here.

(CARTER and MAX ponder this)

KENDRA
Thank you. Point proven.

MAX
We talk about other things.

KENDRA
Yeah? Like what?

MAX
The girls Carter's sleeping with.

(Beat. MAX didn't mean to say that; it was just the first thing that came to his mind)

CARTER
And...you know. Other stuff.

MAX
But we don't talk about that. Anymore. 'Cause you two...you're all....Cartendra.

KENDRA
Did you just give us a celebrity couple name?

(Beat)

MAX
...no...

CARTER
Star Wars was just how we met. We have lives outside of it.

KENDRA
He's got an R2D2 dog costume. But he does not have a dog.

MAX
Weren't you like a film student or something?

KENDRA
Film major. And I graduated.

MAX
See, that's what I don't get. How can you call yourself a film person and not love the Star Wars movies?

KENDRA
Because they're flawed.

(The sounds of running footsteps upstairs. DAVE bursts into the room)

DAVE
What did she say?

CARTER
The new ones suck, I'll give you that...

MAX
Hey, the Obi-Wan/Vader fight in Revenge of the Sith was awesome.

DAVE
Three words-Computer. Animated. Yoda.

MAX
They had to! No way could an ancient Muppet jump around like that.

DAVE
Yoda shouldn't have to jump around at all! He's 900 years old!

CARTER
Hon, you were trying to make a point.

KENDRA
Yes, thank you. My point is, these movies have some serious problems.

DAVE
No! You just...NO!

KENDA
First off, have you actually listened to that dialogue? I mean, it sounds like a freaking Mad Lib.

CARTER
OK, come on now...

KENDRA
And I'm sorry, but thematically, some of it just doesn't work.

MAX
You're so wrong! How can you be so wrong!?

KENDRA
Let's talk about Jabba's palace.

DAVE
Oooooooh, yes. Please. Let's talk about it.

CARTER
Is this about that crappy CGI Jabba they put in A New Hope? 'Cause I think we all agree that thing sucked.

MAX & DAVE
Yes.

KENDRA
No, I'm talking about Revenge of the Jedi.

DAVE
Return! RETURN of the Jedi!

KENDRA
Fine! Revenge, Return, Rehash...whatever! The part where they bust Harrison Ford out of the palace in the desert. So they all go in, their plan falls to complete shit, but they manage to kill all the bad guys, who outnumber them like 20-to-1, rescue their pal, and escape without a scratch.

DAVE
Yes. Epic heroism.

KENDRA
Empty heroism.

DAVE
Excuse me?

KENDRA
It was a walk in the park for these people. It didn't cost them anything! That isn't heroism, it's meaningless.

DAVE
This is just...am I really getting film criticism from the girl who sells gummy bears at the Cineplex?!

KENDRA
Mmm. I can feel how much you hate this, knowing I'm totally right.

DAVE
No!

KENDRA
Like honey on my lips.

DAVE
You...there's this whole, like, societal context you're not taking into account. In 1984...

KENDRA
All I'm saying is, when I saw that movie, I saw flawless stereotypes, not human beings.

MAX
Um, technically, Chewbacca isn't a human being; He's a Wookie. So...yeah.

DAVE
(Standing there, sputtering with rage) I...you... How can.... *(He tries to calm himself down)* OK. OK. Just breathe in... *(He returns)* Carter, are you sure you want it involved in this?

KENDRA
Alright, assbag. If you call me "it" one more time...

DAVE
You'll do what? Viciously evaluate my through-line?

CARTER
OK! Got that out of your system? 'Cause we're not having this fight on the job, and I'm not leaving either of you behind. There will be NO changes, not fifteen minutes before we start!

MAX
Then you're not gonna want to see your mask.

CARTER
What?

DAVE
Max, shut up.

CARTER
What's he talking about?

MAX
Dave is making us wear ski masks.

(Beat)

CARTER
What else would we wear?

MAX
We were supposed to wear the other masks! Remember? I was gonna be Chewie, you were gonna be Han, Dave was gonna be Luke and...

KENDRA
No. No. Don't you dare say I was supposed to be Princess Leia.

MAX
Well, not anymore! Dave didn't get the masks.

CARTER
Max, buddy...just calm down. This doesn't change anything at all. The plan still goes ahead exactly as...planned, OK? I promise, it's gonna work no matter what masks we wear.

MAX
OK.

CARTER
Good. Dave, the files.

DAVE
Right. *(He grabs the files, starts to hand them out)* So I tried to clean these up as best I could, but...

KENDRA
Oh my god. This thing reeks.

CARTER
OK. Basics. Max, you got the truck.

MAX
Yep. No paper trail either.

CARTER
Fake plates?

MAX
Fake plates.

CARTER
And the bikes?

MAX
Suzuki Katanas, just like we've been practicing on.

CARTER
Full tanks?

MAX
Yeah. I got receipts for that...

CARTER
OK, folks. Open 'em up.

(They all open their files)

KENDRA
Oh lord. It smells worse on the inside.

CARTER
Talk us through this, Dave. What we got?

DAVE
Ok. This is pretty simple, people. No major changes here.

CARTER
Go through it again. Every detail. I want this fresh in our minds.

DAVE
OK. We leave the house at... *(He points to MAX)*

MAX
Ten thirty.

DAVE
Because... *(He points to KENDRA)*

KENDRA
Because security goes through their night rotation at eleven.

DAVE
Right. We're going to take the short cut there, down Lawson Road.

KENDRA
No way. Have you seen the potholes on Lawson?

CARTER
We can do it. I take Lawson all the time, to cut down the commute.

KENDRA
It's impossible, even for a commuter!

DAVE
Once we get to the entrance... *(Puts a large dart gun on the table. CARTER takes it, examining it)*

KENDRA
Whoa.

DAVE
Standard zookeeper-issue trank gun.

CARTER
We pull the van up, I nail the gate guard with this. It'll take him out of the equation. And then I take his keys.

MAX
Will it hurt him?

CARTER
He'll just take a very deep nap. Poor guy'll probably make employee of the month.

KENDRA
That gate looks pretty small. You sure you can get through it?

MAX
Totally. It's like 2 meters wide.

KENDRA
Meters? Did we just fall into Canada?

(DAVE rolls out a slide projector while they talk. He shows them their plan thru slides)

DAVE
We'll penetrate their defenses, here... (He points at the projection) And...ok, first thing you'll find in the files is a detailed map of the Kenner Toys Warehouse Facility, provided by our own Carter Sloan...

CARTER
Thank you.

KENDRA
Wait. Kenner? 'Cause your badge says Mattel...

CARTER
Baby, it's a Kenner Warehouse. And when Mattel

bought them out a few years back...

KENDRA
Right.

MAX
Stay on target, stay on target...

DAVE
I've mapped out our in-routes on page one, our out-routes on page 2. Let's go over the in. Once the gate guard is blissfully unconscious, we'll take the main route straight to Warehouse number 6...

KENDRA
And you're sure no one will try and stop us?

DAVE
What did we just go over? Security will be rotating. Once inside, we drive around to the Southern side of the warehouse, where we'll find the loading dock.

KENDRA
Where is that?

CARTER
(Leaning in, showing it to her on the map) Right.....
there.

DAVE
Once we're at #6, Carter, you'll have to work your magic. *(He tosses CARTER an ID badge)*

CARTER
This is it, huh?

DAVE
Absolutely.

MAX
What is it?

DAVE
My piece de resistance. Say hello to Luke Georgus, newest Senior VP at Mattel.

KENDRA
Luke Georgus? Really?

DAVE
Pretty great, right?

KENDRA
That's just...the definition of awful.

DAVE
No one cares what you think.

CARTER
I care.

KENDRA
I'm just saying that name is gonna raise a few flags.

DAVE
You're over-thinking it! It doesn't matter what the name is, only that the card has Level 10 clearance! Obviously, Carter's lame stockboy badge wouldn't get him very far...

CARTER
Hey. Being a lame stock boy got us this far.

DAVE
Yes. Absolutely. Your insider knowledge has been invaluable. But the fact is, we can't have your ID number showing up on the computer records. So I invented Luke Georgus!

MAX
I actually think it's pretty funny.

DAVE
I hacked into their database, determined what sort of protocols they use, and...voila. The result of my very hard work and several hundreds of dollars is a badge that will get us in, out, and never ever be traced to any of us. You know how to use it?

CARTER
Yep.

DAVE
After you swipe it, it'll ask you for your pass-code. It's 05251977.

(The guys all laugh)

KENDRA
What? What's so funny?

CARTER
That's when Star Wars first opened, baby. May 25, 1977.

KENDRA
(Resting her head in her hands) Oh lord.

MAX
Come on! That's awesome!

KENDRA
You betcha.

DAVE
OK, OK. Once Carter gets us in, what do we do first?

MAX
Get the motorcycles out of the back.

DAVE
Yes. Carter will get the loading dock open, then
we run in and...

CARTER
And there it is. The motherlode.

MAX
Oh man. I...I can't even imagine it.

CARTER
Pretty soon, you won't have to.

MAX
Every one, right? Every single one?

CARTER
In mint condition, in boxes. 6 or more copies of
each.

DAVE
All the original Star Wars collection. Kendra,
you'll find pictures of them in your file.

KENDRA
Why?

DAVE
Because you might not recognize them on
sight.

KENDRA
I know what a Star Wars toy looks like.

DAVE
Collectibles. And forgive me, but I trust your
relevant knowledge.

MAX
I don't trust it either.

CARTER
She is my girlfriend.

KENDRA
Did we or did we not just see a bunch of them in
that cabinet there?

CARTER
It's gonna be what you saw there times 10.

MAX
Awesome. Freakin' awesome.

CARTER
I know. The first time my boss showed it to me, I
nearly pissed my pants. And it's not just Star Wars.
It's every toy Kenner ever made. Gargoyles, Silver
Hawks, Stretch Armstrong...

MAX
You're kidding! Stretch Armstrong? For real?

CARTER
And Stretch Ninja and Stretch Monster and all
of them. Lots and lots of every single one. There
were at least 7 copies of the original 1977 Luke
Skywalker.

DAVE
Telescoping lightsaber?

CARTER
Oh yes. That's right. Telescoping Lightsaber.

KENDRA
Back on track, please.

DAVE
Right. Once the bikes are out of the truck, we're
gonna have to move fast. We start with the big

boys-Vehicles, Playsets, Monsters...anything in a large box. We stack those along the bottom.

KENDRA
Monsters?

DAVE
Jabba the Hutt. The Rancor. The Wampa. Keep up. Once all the big boxes are loaded up...and I do mean all. Are we clear on that? No collectible is to be left behind.

CARTER
Got it.

KENDRA
Yes.

MAX
What if we're running out of time?

DAVE
Shouldn't be an issue. I've got this thing planned down to the minute. We'll go faster if we set up a line. Carter, you'll be first because you know the place. Followed by Kendra, then me, then Max. You'll be at the truck loading things up. It's got to be fast but safe.

MAX
Heavy collectibles on bottom, light on top.

DAVE
Exactly. After the boxes are clear, we move on to action figures. Each of you will be given a heavy duty garbage bag, but-and I cannot emphasize this enough-they are NOT to be used unless we run out of time. These action figure packages are very delicate, and we need to handle them accordingly.

The difference between Mint and Near Mint may not look like much, but it can cost us plenty. However, if the clock is running down, bust out the bags. Get as many action figures in them as you can and go. In particular, any Yak-Faces, Blue Snaggletooths...

KENDRA
Shouldn't that be "Snaggleteeth?"

DAVE
No. Shut up. In your packets, I've highlighted the really, REALLY rare ones. They are priority. Got it?

CARTER
Got it.

DAVE
Once everything is loaded up, the three of us hop on the motorcycles.

MAX
OK. I don't get that part. Explain it again.

DAVE
1) We can't all fit in the van after it's full of stolen booty. 2) If-and this is a huuuuge if, because there's no chance it will happen-but IF something bad happened, and the police got involved, they'd be chasing four people instead of one. So, as you'll all see on page 5, I've mapped out alternate routes for all of you. We all go in different directions, and meet back here at one. If you have to shake someone on your tail, do it. Get back here when you can.

(MAX is starting to really freak out)

DAVE
I'm not trying to freak you out with this, dude. I just have to have all the contingencies covered. You understand, right?

(MAX nods)

DAVE
Besides, you'll be in the van. And is there a single person in the city who knows the back-alleys and shortcuts like you? All those years of driving moving trucks are about to pay off, my friend.

CARTER
It was all leading up to this.

MAX
I...I can do this. Right?

CARTER
Buddy, I wouldn't have asked you if I thought for a second that you couldn't.

MAX
Thanks, man. I won't let you down. I promise.

DAVE
Once we get back here, we inventory what we've got. You all have a list of each and every Star Wars collectible Kenner made from 1977 to present. We need to know how many of each we've got. Then...

KENDRA
Then I make the call.

(Beat)

DAVE
Yes. Then you make the call. From this.

(He shows her a phone connected to a strange device next to his computer)

KENDRA
Um...what kind of freaky, mutant nerd-phone is that?

DAVE
The kind that'll bounce the call across twenty different sources. Anyone trying to trace it will get a whole lot of nothing.

KENDRA
Where the hell do you get this stuff? James Bond-R-Us?

DAVE
Guess what? You don't need to know. Now shut up.

CARTER
Dude!

DAVE
(To KENDRA) You're the one who's been in touch with this guy. He understands what we want?

(KENDRA says nothing)

DAVE
Hello? I'm asking you a question.

KENDRA
I'm sorry. I was confused. I thought you just told me to shut up. Ass.

(DAVE glares at her, fuming)

KENDRA
Yes. My contact is well aware of what we're asking

and how we're asking for it. 2 million dollars in
unmarked, non-sequential bills. I make the call,
we determine a hand-off spot, and the deal's done.

DAVE
Here. We do the hand-off here.

KENDRA
Slow down, twitchy. We haven't decided on
anything yet.

CARTER
No, it's a good idea. When we do this, we want
to have the advantage. Best way to get that is
on home ground. We let them pick the spot and
we're just asking them to screw us over.

(KENDRA considers this)

KENDRA
Yeah. Yeah, ok.

(DAVE is about to say something, but KENDRA
interrupts him)

KENDRA
Don't ask.

DAVE
But...

KENDRA
The less you know about this guy, the better. He's
good for the 2 million, and he won't welch.

MAX
So you know him pretty well?

KENDRA
Yeah, I do.

DAVE
Look, I have spent a lot of time getting this whole operation together, and I gotta tell you, this unknown element is...I mean, who the hell are we dealing with here? Some insanely wealthy Star Wars Fanatic. That's all we know.

KENDRA
I told you guys from the beginning. My client prefers to remain anonymous. I'm the go-between, and if you want your big ol' pile of money, then you need to get real comfortable with that.

MAX
Dave's got a point. We got a good plan here, but we're taking a big leap of faith.

CARTER
Trust her, guys.

DAVE
Why? Give me one good reason.

CARTER
Because I said so.

(Beat)

MAX
Yeah. Yeah, OK.

DAVE
Alright.

CARTER
Good. Let's suit up. *(He passes out some surgical latex gloves)* Put these on first. You'll still have full range of motion and sensation, but no pesky fingerprints. Now these-- *(He produces a duffle bag, and pulls out four jumpsuits. As they talk,*

everyone puts them on)

MAX
Where'd you get these?

CARTER
Somewhere where no one will miss them. Once the deed is done and we're far away from the Warehouses, take these and ditch them somewhere inconspicuous. Then, we can come back here. But leave the gloves on. Don't touch anything with your bare hands till we're clear. Got it?

DAVE
Absolutely.

KENDRA
Sure.

MAX
Yeah.

CARTER
Good. Dave, mask us.

(DAVE hands everyone their ski-masks)

KENDRA
Oh thank god.

(The following dialogue occurs as they dress)

MAX
Hey. Hey, Carter.

CARTER
What'cha gonna do with the money? *(He stares at KENDRA for a second)*

MAX
Dave and I were talking about it before and...

CARTER
Gonna rent out a recording studio, cut my first album.

MAX
For real?! Like for Funk Force or...?

CARTER
No, man. Solo Album. The Carter Sloan Experience. Time for this Millennium Falcon to spread his wings and fly, you know?

DAVE
Um, the Millennium Falcon didn't have wings, per se.

KENDRA
Oh my god...

MAX
Dude, that's so awesome.

DAVE
I mean, erroneous metaphor aside, it really is.

CARTER
Right?

MAX
I thought for sure you and Kendra would, like, go off somewhere and...

KENDRA
(First to finish dressing) Done.

DAVE
It's not a race, Kendra.

CARTER
Guys, stop sniping at each other.

DAVE
I'm not sniping. She's sniping.

KENDRA
Your mom's sniping.

CARTER
OK. What you guys are doing, right now, is sniping. Knock it off.

MAX
(sing-song) You guys got in trou-ble...

(They are now all fully outfitted. MAX stares at all of them and starts to laugh)

MAX
Look at us, man. We're criminals. We are criminals!

DAVE
Hell yeah!

CARTER
Hell yeah!

KENDRA
Fuckin' A!

(Beat)

KENDRA
Hell yeah.

CARTER
Seating arrangements-Max, you're driving. I'm in the passenger seat. Dave, you and Kendra are in the back with the bikes.

DAVE
What?

KENDRA
No. No way. I'll ride shotgun.

CARTER
No can do, baby. I gotta be up front so I can peg the guard. And Max has gotta be behind the wheel. So suck it up. Both of you.

(DAVE stares at KENDRA. She stares at him)

DAVE
I don't like you.

KENDRA
I don't like you either.

DAVE
But I can honestly say, we could not have done this without you.

(He offers his hand. She smiles a sly smile)

KENDRA
You got that right.

(She shakes his hand)

DAVE
OK then.

(Beat. This is the moment, and they all know it)

CARTER
All right, guys. This is it. The point of no return. You all know what we're trying to do, but here's where I say it out loud. If we walk out these doors, we're gonna be robbing a multi-billion dollar corporation of something more precious than gold. If we get caught, we're fucked, plain and simple. But if we trust each other, if we trust that

we've all done our parts to perfection, then we will not be caught. *(Beat)* Guys, I don't... *(Takes a breath)* Look at us. We've known each other pretty much all our lives. When we were on that playground 30 years ago, did you ever think we'd end up here? Think back to all the dreams we had back then. Everything we wanted to achieve. And look at us now. We haven't achieved a damn thing. That's why we are where we are right now. We've been given an incredible gift. Most people like us...they don't ever get this chance. A chance to fix everything. No more living in your mother's basement, watching the world go by through a web-cam. No more trying to raise a kid by yourself, wondering how you're going to afford one more day. No more working at a movie theatre, wishing you were behind the camera instead of the ticket counter. And... *(He takes KENDRA's hand)* And no more living like a teenager, working a teenager's job and bouncing from one girl to the next. I don't want to do that anymore. I...just can't. I want something better than that. And so do all of you. We were kids once, and we saw the world with different eyes. But we forgot about that. We got so hung up by how we thought the world was, that we forgot what it could be. Our lives don't have to be like this. All we need is a chance, and enough courage to take it. Is it a huge risk? Yes. Do we all have something to lose? Absolutely. But let's face the truth. We've all lost too much already. Now, we have an opportunity to take something back. Our fates. Our lives. They can be ours again. I don't know about you, but I think that's worth it. I know it is.

(Everyone takes this in. Finally--)

MAX
So do I.
DAVE
Me too.

KENDRA
I love you so much.

(She and CARTER kiss)

CARTER
Then let's do it. Let's change our lives.

(The gang rushes up the stairs excitedly. Lights fade to black)

END OF ACT I

ACT II

(Lights up. The basement. No one is present, with the possible exception of Spencer. We hear a van pull up. After a brief moment, we hear MAX running through the house)

MAX
(Offstage) Oh man, oh man, oh man, oh man...

(The door opens and MAX runs down the stairs. He is alone, no longer wearing his mask or jumpsuit, though he still has his gloves on)

MAX
Guys, what the... *(Looks around, realizing he's alone)* Guys?

(He tears through the apartment, looking for them. His nervousness is verging on hysteria)

MAX
No, no, no. C'mon, guys...

(The phone by the computer begins to ring. MAX

freezes in utter terror)

MAX
Oh boy. Phone's ringing.

(It rings three times, then is silent. MAX collapses in a chair, breathing heavily. After a few seconds, the phone begins to ring again. His head rises, frightened eyes slowly moving to the phone)

MAX
What the hell is goin' on?

(MAX slowly goes to the phone. He reaches to answer it, and picks up the receiver. Then, he hangs it back up and takes it off the base. He paces the room like a frightened child, mumbling to himself. He either finds Spencer or pretends to see him hiding under something)

MAX
Spencer? Come here, buddy. Gooood kitty. Now, listen to me carefully. I need you to go outside and find Carter and Dave, ok? Can you do that, Spencer? *(He hears a motorcycle pull up)* Oh, thank you, Jesus. *(He waits anxiously)*

(KENDRA runs down the stairs)

KENDRA
Thank god you guys got... *(She looks around, realizing that MAX is the only one there)* Where are they?

MAX
I don't know! How the hell should I know!? I'm not in charge!

KENDRA
OK, OK. Calm down. We have to...

MAX
What about Dave? What about Carter?! There were gunshots! There were security guards and... *(He grabs KENDRA by the shoulders, shaking her in a rising panic)* WHAT THE HELL IS GOING ON!?

(KENDRA punches MAX hard in the face, sending him flying)

KENDRA
Don't you touch me, you fat piece of crap! I don't know what happened! I just drove off when it all went to hell. You're the first person I've seen since we scattered.

MAX
You haven't seen Carter?

KENDRA
No. Once those guys started shooting I...oh...oh god...what if...?

MAX
No. No way. Not Carter.

KENDRA
Who were those guys? They came out of nowhere.

MAX
Security guards, I think.

KENDRA
We were only there maybe five minutes.

MAX
They probably saw the gate guard with a freaking dart in his neck and flipped out!

KENDRA
But they just shot at us! They didn't tell us to give up or anything. Isn't that what they're supposed to do? In the movies, they always say "freeze" or something...

MAX
That's it. I gotta...I...see ya.

(*MAX heads for the stairs. KENDRA stops him*)

KENDRA
Where are you going?

MAX
I'm gonna find Carter and Dave.

KENDRA
What? How?

MAX
I'm gonna drive around until I catch up with them.

KENDRA
Oh my god. Are you actually as stupid as I think you are?

MAX
What?

KENDRA
You can't go cruising around in a vehicle that the cops might be looking for! Just leave it behind the house.

MAX
My friends are out there! Your boyfriend!

KENDRA
And they'll be here any minute. Just wait.

MAX
We can't just do nothing.

KENDRA
Nothing is exactly what we're gonna do. You got that?

(MAX says nothing)

KENDRA
That wasn't a rhetorical question! You got it!?

MAX
Yes!

KENDRA
Good. Because the last thing we need to do right now is come apart. You don't like me, and god knows I don't like you, but we are in this together. OK?

MAX
Yeah. Yeah, OK.

KENDRA
OK. *(Walks into the bathroom, and proceeds to vomit. She comes out in a bit, and collapses into a chair)* OK. That's better. Did you get anything?

MAX
Collectibles?

KENDRA
Yeah.

MAX
(Shakes his head) You?

KENDRA
No. We barely got the doors open before those guys showed up.

MAX
Maybe they weren't security guards. Maybe they were black ops or something.

KENDRA
They weren't black ops.

MAX
You don't know.

KENDRA
Why would the government send black ops after us, idiot?

MAX
Maybe...one of the chiefs of staff...likes...toys.

KENDRA
Can you even hear yourself?

MAX
Shut up.

(The sound of a motorcycle pulling up)

KENDRA
Dammit...

MAX
Wait.

KENDRA
Nuh-uh. We gotta get out of here.

MAX
Just listen to that, will you?

(Beat. They listen)

MAX
That's a Katana.

KENDRA
A what?

MAX
It's one of our bikes, you...girl.

KENDRA
Like you know. A motorcycle is a motorcycle.

(MAX stares at her)

KENDRA
What?

MAX
I have no idea what he sees in you.

KENDRA
Excuse me?

MAX
Nothing. Forget it.

KENDRA
You want to know what he sees in me? I'll tell you what he...

(The door opens. KENDRA jumps up)

KENDRA
Carter?

(DAVE comes down the stairs)

KENDRA
Oh.

MAX
Thank you, Jesus. *(MAX embraces DAVE, who hugs him back somewhat weakly)* Oh man. I thought you were...

KENDRA
Where's Carter?

MAX
Are you OK?

DAVE
A bullet...

MAX
What?

KENDRA
I said "Where's..."

MAX
Not you.

DAVE
A bullet...right past my face. I saw it. It was so close. Like everything was slow motion.

KENDRA
Did you see Carter?

DAVE
(Shaking his head) I don't even remember how I got to the motorcycle. How I got here. I just... everything's all flooey.

MAX
Do you need to puke? Kendra puked.

DAVE
OK.

(DAVE calmly walks into the bathroom and vomits)

MAX
Better?

DAVE
My teeth feel fuzzy.

KENDRA
I think he's in shock.

MAX
How do you know? You work at a movie theatre.

KENDRA
Yeah. Which means I watch a lot of movies. This is what people are like when they're in shock. *(She grabs DAVE's face)* Dave, I need you to look at me, OK?

DAVE
OK.

KENDRA
Are you hurt?

DAVE
No. I don't think so. No blood.

KENDRA
Good. That's good. Now listen to me, Dave. This is very important. Where-Is-Carter?

DAVE
I have no idea.

KENDRA
(To Max) He's useless.

MAX
Get away from him. *(MAX goes to DAVE)* It's gonna be just fine, buddy.

DAVE
What?

MAX
I said "It's gonna be..."

(DAVE starts laughing. Quietly at first, then growing in intensity)

MAX
Uh...Dave?

DAVE
Are you mental? "Ok?" "OK?!" Were you even there?!

MAX
Of course I...

DAVE
They came out of nowhere. They had guns! They shot at us before we...I ran. I'm sorry, but I did. Not at first. First, I just...kind of did nothing. I think maybe I peed a little. And then, I...

KENDRA
We know what you did.

DAVE
Yeah? Well, what did you do?

(KENDRA says nothing)

DAVE
Yeah, that's right. You can sit there and call me useless, but what did you do when those guys showed up? Huh? I can't hear you, Kendra! What the hell did you do?

KENDRA
Look, I just...

DAVE
You ran! You jumped on your motorcycle and you

ran off! You didn't even think about Carter, did you? You were too busy cryin' for your mama!

KENDRA
Shut up! Shut up!

(KENDRA pulls out CARTER's gun)

MAX
Oh Jesus!

DAVE
Whoa. Slow down there.

KENDRA
This wasn't supposed to happen, ok?! Your plan was supposed to work! This isn't my fault. You must have tripped an alarm or something.

DAVE
Kendra, just put the gun down.

KENDRA
I don't even remember how I got this. It's all a huge blur. What the hell happened, Dave? We've been working on this for months. We had everything planned, and...

DAVE
I know.

KENDRA
I want Carter. Where's Carter? You should have been looking out for him. He trusted you guys and now he....he...I want Carter...

(KENDRA is on the verge of tears. Suddenly, the basement door swings open. Everyone jumps, and KENDRA points the gun at the door)

KENDRA
Who is it? Who's there?

(There's no answer)

KENDRA
I said "Who's there"?!

(CARTER steps onto the stairs, pale and moving slowly)

MAX
Oh god.

KENDRA
Carter?

CARTER
...I feel terrible...

(With that, CARTER tumbles down the stairs. They all run to him, and MAX lifts him off the ground)

KENDRA
Oh my god! Is he OK? What's going on?!

MAX
Oh man, oh man, oh man...

(DAVE turns to run)

KENDRA
Get back here!

DAVE
We need to lie him down!

MAX
Hurry! He's bleeding!

KENDRA
What?

MAX
I think he's been shot.

CARTER
I have been shot.

KENDRA
Oh my god!

(DAVE makes a large sitting area out of beanbags. They gently lay CARTER down)

DAVE
Hang in there, dude. I'm gonna go get some bandages.

CARTER
Awesome.

KENDRA
Baby? Where were you...?

CARTER
Help me get my coat off.

(They remove his jacket, and his arm is covered in blood)

MAX
Oh....jeez...

CARTER
AH! DAMMIT!

KENDRA
Honey, you're shot!

CARTER
Really? You think so?!

DAVE
(Returning with towels) Here.

KENDRA
I thought you were getting bandages!

DAVE
Look, this isn't M.A.S.H., OK? We don't have any bandages. This is the best I could find.

CARTER
Could somebody DO SOMETHING!?

DAVE
Yeah, lemme just... *(Presses the towels to the wound)*

CARTER
AAAAAAH! Fuck! Fuck!

KENDRA
What are you doing?!

DAVE
You're supposed to apply pressure, right?

CARTER
Oh God! Stop it!

DAVE
I think I'm supposed to do this!

(MAX pulls DAVE away just as CARTER swings at him)

KENDRA
Are you trying to kill him?!

MAX
Stop yelling!

DAVE
I was trying to staunch the bleeding, you moron!

MAX
Stop!

KENDRA
Staunch? Did you actually use the word "staunch?"

MAX
SHUT UP!!!!

(Everyone is silent)

MAX
Oh man, this is so fucked up.

CARTER
...I think I'm gonna puke...

MAX
We need to get you to a hospital.

CARTER
No. Very bad idea.

(MAX gets close to CARTER, speaking to him as though he's had some sort of head trauma)

MAX
Carter. I need you to listen to me. You have been shot. You've lost a lot of blood, and we have to take you to a hospital so they can make you all better.

CARTER
Max, we can't do that.

MAX
(Turning to DAVE & KENDRA) OK, he's totally out of it.

CARTER
Listen-Hospitals have to call the police anytime they treat a gunshot wound. The minute you walk me though those doors, it's over.

KENDRA
Well, what should we do?

CARTER
I don't know.

DAVE
You've got to think of something.

CARTER
Why do I have to think of everything? I'm the one bleeding on your carpet. You think of something.

DAVE
I don't know. Maybe I can try to take the bullet out myself.

CARTER
(Looks to KENDRA) You think of something!

DAVE
Oh! Wait! I've got it! We call your contact.

KENDRA
What?

DAVE
This guy has 2 million dollars to spend on toys. He's gotta have like a private jet or helicopter or something, right?

(KENDRA stares at him, confused)

DAVE
We can fly Carter out of Cincinnati. Hell, out of Ohio entirely. Yeah, yeah. This is good. This is a plan. We call him up, explain the situation...

CARTER
He won't help us. We don't have any collateral.

DAVE

Carter, now's not the time for negative thinking.

CARTER

We botched the job, man. What're we supposed to do? Call him up and say "Hey, we don't have any of your merchandise, and we've got the Cincinnati PD after us, but would you mind if we borrow your private jet and fly to Hawaii?"

MAX

So you didn't get anything either, huh?

CARTER

Oh, I got something. I got a fucking bullet lodged in my fucking bicep!

MAX

But no action figures?

CARTER

NO!

MAX

Hey, don't yell at me! I'm just trying to put this all together, man! I mean, we gotta figure out just how botched we are. *(Turns to DAVE)* Oh! Wait! Did you get anything?

(DAVE is silent)

MAX

Dave?

(No answer)

MAX

Is this part of being in shock? 'Cause I thought he was...

KENDRA
What is it, Bullanksi? What did you get?

DAVE
(Sits down) OK. It happened like this. When we got inside the warehouse....that's when it all started. We were there maybe, what? Two minutes? Something like that. Then the guards showed up. They started shooting and...

KENDRA
Yeah, we were there, remember?

DAVE
So there was gunfire, and...I froze. I thought for sure I was dead. I saw everyone scatter, and I just stood there. Suddenly, I dropped. It was the only thing I could think to do. I dropped to the ground, and crawled underneath the aisles. Thousands of dollars of collectibles above me, and I just crawled. I made it to the end of the aisle, and there was this door. It was just tucked in a corner, it wasn't even on the building schematics. Then I remembered. Carter gave me the guard's keys. Remember?

CARTER
Yeah, I was sick of carrying them. They kept poking my nuts.

DAVE
So I figure, maybe there's a window or something I can crawl out of. So I get in, and lock it behind me. And inside, I...there was... *(DAVE becomes misty, lost in the memory)* It wasn't a big room. Really, just a closet. The only thing in it was a safe. One of the old tumbler models. And I...I don't know. I felt this presence...this pull.

And the next thing I knew, I had my ear pressed to the door, my fingers on the dial.

KENDRA
Wait, you can jimmy a safe?

DAVE
It was more than that. It was like something was guiding my hands. Before I knew it...the door swung open and...there it was...a...a...

(DAVE is lost in the emotion of the moment. MAX gently pats his shoulder)

DAVE
It was amazing. It was real. And now, it's mine.

KENDRA
What? What is yours?

(DAVE pulls his garbage bag out from under his shirt. There is a single, boxed Star Wars figure. The others crowded around DAVE, even CARTER. MAX and CARTER stare at it as though they have witnessed the Holy Grail. They are on the verge of tears. KENDRA is confused and unimpressed)

MAX
Oh...oh my lord...

CARTER
No way, dude. No way.

DAVE
It's true.

KENDRA
What is it?

CARTER
The Holy Grail.

KENDRA
No, it's a toy.

MAX
Kendra, I know you're wrong a lot, but you've never been more wrong than you are right now.

KENDRA
What? It's that bounty hunter guy. Robo something.

DAVE
BOBA Fett. Now, look hard at this particular action figure. In your mind, compare it to the print-outs I gave you of all known existing Action Figures.

KENDRA
(Stares at the toy intensely) I'm not following you.

DAVE
What is that by his head?!

KENDRA
His helmet?

DAVE
Yes, his helmet! That's the whole point! He's not wearing his freaking helmet!

KENDRA
I can see he's not wearing his freaking helmet!

CARTER
Honey, you need to understand. What we are looking at is an urban myth...a legend. There was never, ever, EVER a Boba Fett released with a

removable helmet. Ever.

KENDRA
Well, obviously there was. It's right here.

DAVE
Exactly. We're looking at the only one.

KENDRA
Seriously?

DAVE
Yes.

KENDRA
So this is like a one of a kind? No one anywhere has this thing, except us?

DAVE
Yes.

(Beat)

KENDRA
Holy shit.

MAX
Check the copyright.

DAVE
It's legit. 1985.

MAX
Power of the Force series.

DAVE
That's right.

(CARTER topples over)

KENDRA
Oh god! Baby?!

MAX
OH CRAP!!!! HE'S DEAD!!!!

DAVE
He's not dead! He just passed out from blood loss.

KENDRA
Carter...

MAX
Blood loss leads to death, David!

KENDRA
Do something!

DAVE
Get him back on those bean bags. We need something to use for bandages.

(KENDRA goes to the closet)

DAVE
What are you doing?

KENDRA
Tearing up sheets. Bandages, like you said.

(She pulls out some Star Wars sheets. She is about to tear them. MAX & DAVE both stop her)

DAVE
Whoa, whoa, whoa!

MAX
Not those!

DAVE
Seriously. Chill out. I have other sheets.

(DAVE grabs other sheets and tears them himself. MAX gently ties them over CARTER's arm. KENDRA sits with him)

MAX
Hang in there, buddy.

KENDRA
OK. We're making a plan, right now. Gimme the phone. I'm calling my guy.

DAVE
I thought we threw that plan out.

KENDRA
That was before we had collateral.

(Beat)

DAVE
What exactly are you talking about here?

KENDRA
The Holy Grail. That'll give us some leverage with...

DAVE
Excuse me? We're not putting this up on the chopping block.

KENDRA
Carter is bleeding to death! We're gonna do what we've got to do.

DAVE
By giving up the greatest find in Collector history? You have completely lost sight of what this whole thing is about!

KENDRA
Give me the doll, Dave.

DAVE
Max, you're with me, right?

MAX
I gotta be honest. I'm feeling pretty conflicted.

DAVE
Look. You guys aren't thinking clearly. There's a lot of emotion involved, and I can sympathize with that. I really can. But you've got to look at this realistically. This action figure changes everything. We have to keep it. And Carter would agree with me if he was conscious.

KENDRA
Excuse me?

DAVE
You don't understand! None of you understand! This isn't just some piece of merchandise! It's so much bigger than that...than us. What do you think this is, huh? *(He points to his collection)* You think it's some weird aspect of my obsession. But it isn't. It's a temple. A sanctuary for what we should be...what we've lost sight of. A better world. A world built on hope and faith and honor. A world far, far away. And now, we can be led back to it.

KENDRA
What, by you?

DAVE
No. By him. *(He holds up the toy)*

KENDRA
(To MAX) Get 'im.

(Beat)

MAX
What?

KENDRA
I said "get 'im." And you're supposed to, I don't know, tackle him or something.

MAX
But he's my best friend.

KENDRA
What about Carter?! Remember him? The unconscious guy on the beanbags?

DAVE
Max, listen to me.

(CARTER rouses, incoherent. He sings a Funk Force song)

CARTER
…Baby, just pull the lever…rock 'n roll's gonna live forever…

KENDRA
Carter? Are you ok?

CARTER
…gonna live…FOREVER….

KENDRA
Honey, don't…

DAVE
I hate that song.

MAX
Dude, that's their hit!

KENDRA
Max, look at him. This is not normal.

DAVE
He's getting delirious.

CARTER
No, I'm not. Your face is...the one that's...shut up...

KENDRA
All right, to hell with you. I'm calling my contact.

DAVE
No!

(DAVE closes in on her, KENDRA pulls the gun and points it right at him)

KENDRA
I wouldn't.

DAVE
Max, we have to...

(She cocks her gun)

KENDRA
Seriously. I wouldn't.

(They freeze. She reaches to the phone)

KENDRA
It's off the hook.

(Beat)

KENDRA
Why is it off the hook?

MAX
Yeah. Um...funny story...

KENDRA
Is it, fat boy? Is it a funny story? 'Cause I gotta tell ya, I could use a freaking laugh at this point. Everything's pretty much been a big downer so far. So start talking. Don't hold back. Regale me.

(Beat)

MAX
It's...it's not that kind of funny.

KENDRA
(barely restraining her rage) Tell. Me. Anyway.

MAX
Well, it's like this...

DAVE
Kendra, do not make that call.

KENDRA
Was I talking to you, freakshow? No! I was not talking to you, so shut the hell up already. Let fat boy talk.

MAX
So when I got here, the phone was ringing. A lot. Like every minute, someone just kept calling and calling...

KENDRA
Who?

MAX
I don't know. I took the phone off the hook.

KENDRA
Why would you do that?

(CARTER quietly sings a guitar riff as they fight)

MAX
I don't know! I panicked! What do you want me to say? All hell broke loose, and I didn't know if you guys were alive or dead, and the phone was ringing, and...

KENDRA
OK. Chill out. I guess it's fine. We'll just...

(As soon as she puts the phone on the hook, the phone begins to ring. They all stare at it for a long time, silent and terrified. Finally--)

CARTER
...gonna live FOREVER...

MAX
Aren't you gonna get it?

KENDRA
Why don't you get it?

(DAVE runs into the bathroom)

KENDRA
Hey! What are you...?

(The sound of DAVE vomiting)

KENDRA
(to MAX) Yeah, thank god he's on our side. *(KENDRA takes a breath, then finally picks up the phone)* H...hello? *(Listens)* Yes. This is Kendra.

CARTER
...Forever!...

(MAX starts to pace, freaking out. CARTER passes out again)

KENDRA
Yes.
Yes.
No.
I understand.
Well, it might not be a total...
Ok. Yes, sir.

Wait. How do you...
No, I'm sorry.
Please. Listen to me.
We have something you're gonna want.

MAX
Don't say that!

KENDRA
I mean, really REALLY want.
Yes. I understand.
All right. *(She hangs up the phone)*

MAX
What did you do that for!? We weren't supposed...

KENDRA
He's coming.

MAX
What?

KENDRA
He's coming. Here. Right now.

MAX
Who exactly are we talking about here?

KENDRA
My contact. The guy who was gonna buy all the toys.

MAX
You mean the toys we don't have!

KENDRA
It's done, Max. Deal with it.

MAX
Oh god. I gotta sit down. I think I'm gonna have a heart attack.

KENDRA
You're not gonna have a heart attack, you freaking...

(KENDRA collects herself)

KENDRA
Just keep it together, OK. We're gonna be fine.
We've still got that super-rare thingy. That'll be
worth something. Right?

MAX
Yeah. I guess so.

KENDRA
Exactly. So you just sit there and stop spazzing out.
I'm gonna go get Dave. *(She goes to the bathroom,
opening the door as she speaks)* OK, Dave. We need
to... *(She looks in the bathroom. Slowly, her head
lowers in soul-crushing defeat)* Max?

MAX
Yeah?

KENDRA
We have a problem.

MAX
Yeah, I think Carter passed out again. We need to...

KENDRA
You didn't tell me there was a window in the bathroom.

(MAX rises, crossing to her)

MAX
What are you....? *(MAX is next to her, staring into
the bathroom. He is quiet for a moment, then lowers
his head in soul-crushing defeat)* Son of a bitch.

KENDRA
I should have known it. He was in there too long.

MAX
No, no, no. This isn't right. Dave wouldn't run out on us.

KENDRA
Really? 'Cause the big, empty bathroom tells me he did.

(MAX goes in, looking around)

MAX
Dave? Come on, man. This isn't funny.

KENDRA
Hey, check the medicine cabinet. Maybe he's in there.

MAX
He's not! I checked.

(KENDRA goes to CARTER)

KENDRA
Baby, I'm sorry. We fucked up good.

(MAX exits the bathroom)

MAX
OK. He's gone.

KENDRA
I know.

MAX
Well...what are we supposed to do?

KENDRA
I got nothing.

(Beat)

MAX
But...but...we need a plan.

KENDRA
We sure do. But we don't have one.

MAX
We'll ask Carter. When he wakes up. He always has plans. There was this one time, when we were in sixth grade, and it was dodgeball day at gym and...

KENDRA
Carter isn't coming up with anything. He can barely string a thought together.

MAX
Look! Someone's gotta come up with something! And it can't be me! We've always had a clear chain of command, and it goes Carter-Dave-Carter Again-Anyone Else-Spencer-And then me. That's the way it's always been, and I like it that way. So please, I'm begging you...think of something.

KENDRA
Sorry, Max. I'm tapped out.

(MAX collapses on the couch, exhausted)

MAX
I was gonna take my kid to Kings Island tomorrow.

(KENDRA stares at him)

MAX
You know, to celebrate. She loves roller coasters. They scare the hell out of me, but when it's your kid, you kinda...I don't know.

(Beat)

MAX
What were you gonna do?

KENDRA
Tomorrow?

MAX
Yeah.

KENDRA
I...I guess I hadn't thought about it.

MAX
Really?

(She nods)

MAX
I figured you and Carter would like fly somewhere romantic and get engaged or something.

(She laughs)

MAX
What?

KENDRA
I'm not the marrying type, Max.

MAX
Pffft.

KENDRA
Can you picture me all girled up, walking down the aisle?

MAX
Sure. Why not?

(She says nothing)

MAX

Is it because we're always giving you shit? Seriously, that's way more on us than on you.

KENDRA

It's not just you guys. I just...I fight. Anytime I think I need to, I get my fists up.

MAX

Nothing wrong with that.

KENDRA

I know that. But a lot of people would disagree with you.

MAX

Then those people are morons. You know when I knew it was over between me and my wife? When she stopped fighting. She just gave up, on me and Carrie both. Way I figure, if you're fighting...it means you care. *(He realizes that KENDRA is staring at him)* What?

KENDRA

I forget you have a daughter.

(He takes out his wallet and hands it to her)

KENDRA

What's this?

MAX

My daughter Carrie.

(KENDRA looks at it)

KENDRA

Max, that's a picture of Carrie Fisher.

MAX

Next to that one.

KENDRA
Oh.

KENDRA
(Smiles) She's so small.

MAX
Well, she's only four.

KENDRA
She's pretty.

MAX
Yeah.

KENDRA
You look really happy.

MAX
I do?

KENDRA
In the picture.

MAX
Oh.

KENDRA
I thought you only got that way about Star Wars.

MAX
Lady, I'm full of surprises.

KENDRA
Aren't we all?

(Beat)

KENDRA
Did Dave and Carter hate your wife? The way you guys hate me?

MAX
It's not like that. They didn't like her because she made me miserable.

KENDRA
Maybe you guys just don't like sharing your toys.

(MAX stares at her)

KENDRA
Maybe you guys need to just...find your own lives.

MAX
You sound like Mrs. Bullanski.

KENDRA
I mean, I get it. You guys have this comfortable rut. But you could all be more. Carter's this really great bassist and...

MAX
Just...drop it, ok.

KENDRA
I know you guys rely on him to be in charge or whatever, but that's not him, Max. He's not your leader. You guys made him into Han Solo when you were kids, and never saw past it.

MAX
Hey, he wanted to play Han. I was Chewie and...

KENDRA
Of course he did! Everyone wants to be Han Solo! Know who wants to be Luke?

MAX
...Dave?

KENDRA
The ones who are too scared to leave their home

planet.

MAX
Just stop, ok!? We gotta figure out a plan and...

KENDRA
I'm just saying, whatever happens tonight, everything changes.

MAX
Fine! Change is...FINE! But it's not like...we're
friends, Kendra! The kind of friends that...and it's
forever! We're just gonna be friends with money!
I mean, if we can...SEE?! This is why we should
be figuring out a plan instead of...we need a plan!
So just...you don't talk, I won't talk. We're going
to sit here and not say upsetting things and just...
plan. OK?

KENDRA
Max, I'm sorry. I...

MAX
OK!?

KENDRA
OK.

(They sit and think for a bit, staring ahead intently)

KENDRA
I'm coming up empty.

MAX
Me too. *(Beat. MAX turns to her)* Who's your
contact?

(KENDRA says nothing)

MAX
Kendra, this is me trying to make a plan. Help me

out.

(KENDRA says nothing)

MAX
I need you right now. So just give me a name.
Right now. Please!

KENDRA
You don't want to know.

MAX
Me asking means I want to know!

KENDRA
(Grabbing him roughly) Listen to me. Just go
upstairs and get the fuck out of here. Go back to
your daughter, and live a normal life and forget all
about us! Because if you're still here when Big Al
shows up...

MAX
Wait, what?! Big Al? As...as in...?!

KENDRA
Alphonse DiMartino.

MAX
(Stunned and scared) You cannot be serious.

(She nods)

MAX
Al DiMartino? Big Man Al? The mob boss?!

KENDRA
That's right.

MAX
(Backing up) Please tell me you're joking. Tell me
you were not just on the phone with the most

dangerous man in Ohio, and that he's not on his way here right now.

KENDRA
He'll be here in a few minutes.

(MAX sits there in silent terror)

MAX
How the hell do you know Al DiMartino?

(Beat)

KENDRA
We...used to date.

MAX
No way.

KENDRA
Yeah, I used to run with a very different crowd than I do now.

MAX
That...I don't know if that's terrifying or awesome.

KENDRA
(Pacing, her emotions rising) He's rich, y'know! And he's a freaking Star Wars fanatic. And when Carter told me about this...I just...oh god. This is all my fault.

(Beat)

KENDRA
I'm sorry.

(MAX is silent for a bit, conflicted)

MAX
I just...he's a freaking crime lord. Did you really think this was the kind of guy we should be doing

business with?

KENDRA

What was I supposed to do? The whole point was to unload the merchandise fast. The longer we held it, the more likely it would be that...Alphonse had the money. And I knew he'd fork over. You guys think you're obsessed, but he's even worse. You'd think he'd spend his money on drugs or guns or something...No. Star Wars. Everything Star Wars. Original lightsabers. Foreign imports. He's even got two rooms full of all the shit he bought from the original movies.

MAX

You mean, like from the actual movies? You can do that?

KENDRA

If you know the right people. He's got like costumes and masks and all that shit.

MAX

Does...does he have a Chewbacca mask?

KENDRA

Like three of them.

(MAX *is almost moved to tears*)

KENDRA

We met four years ago. Opening night of Attack of the Clones. He bought out the entire theatre at Midnight, the day before it opened. He wanted to watch it alone. My boss offered us double over-time if we'd...I don't know...wait on him. Get him popcorn, refill his drink, shit like that. But we'd have to come to him. Once the movie started, he wasn't leaving. I was the only one who'd do it. I mean, I was scared shitless, but...he was nice. He wasn't creepy or pervy or anything. About halfway through, he just wanted me to sit and watch it with him. Here's this huge, freaking criminal, and he's like a little kid. Afterwards, he took me out for coffee, and...it was nice at first. He was really sweet. I mean, I wasn't stupid, I knew what he did. He never tried to hide it.

MAX
So what happened?

KENDRA
He....we would...god...

MAX
Kendra, what?

KENDRA
He made me...dress up in costumes. When we...y'know. The...

(She mumbles something under her breath. MAX stares at her, unsure)

KENDRA
The Princess Leia slave costume. From Jabba's palace.

(There is a long, uncomfortable silence as neither really knows what to say. Finally--)

MAX
So that's why you hate...

KENDRA
Yes.

MAX
Like with the metal bra and...?

KENDRA
YES.

MAX
OK.

(They are quiet, taking it all in. Suddenly, MAX bursts into action)

MAX
All right. What do we know? We know that we have a big, dangerous crime lord coming here in a few minutes. A crime lord with strange sexual fetishes.

(KENDRA puts her head in her hands)

MAX
Carter is bleeding to death on the beanbags. Dave has run off with the only bargaining chip we had. So...

KENDRA
We're fucked.

MAX
No. Wait. There was this thing I heard once. It's that thing that says the simplest solution is usually the right one.

KENDRA
Occam's Razor.

MAX
What?

KENDRA
That's what the theory's called. Occam's Razor.

(Beat. MAX stares, clearly lost)

KENDRA
Just go on.

MAX
OK. So the situation is bad. We have to get Carter help, which only the Big Man can give us. But he won't do it if we don't have collateral. But we don't have collateral because Dave bolted. That's basically it, right?

KENDRA
Sure, why not?

MAX
So...ok.

(Beat. MAX is silent as he thinks)

MAX
We need collateral. What do we have? *(He looks around, his eyes settling on KENDRA)*

KENDRA
I am not collateral.

MAX
If you really loved Carter...

KENDRA
No.

MAX
Fine.

KENDRA
Oh! Wait! What about that thing!? *(Points at the cabinet)*

MAX
Right! Of course! *(He starts messing with the combination)*

KENDRA
What's the hold up?

MAX
Look, this is a complicated system. For all I know, Dave has it rigged to explode.

KENDRA
Here, let me.

MAX
I can figure it out. I've seen him do it a bunch.

KENDRA
Your fingers are too big.

MAX
My fingers are fine. Shut up.

KENDRA
You're gonna mess it up.

MAX
I'm gonna mess up your face is what I'm gonna mess up.

KENDRA
Nice.

MAX
I can't do it if you...

KENDRA
Just move already!

MAX
You'll set off the alarm, princess!

KENDRA
What'd you call me?

MAX
Would you just...

(The two fall into a slap-fight, like two children. They struggle, but they're more intent on stopping each other than inflicting damage. They manage to get back to the cabinet, still struggling. CARTER rouses himself)

CARTER
Does Dave know you're messing with his stuff?

KENDRA
Honey!

MAX
Take it easy, dude.

CARTER
Gimme some water or something. I'm fallin' apart here.

MAX
Sure. *(Runs to get him some water)*

KENDRA
Baby, don't try to move, OK?

CARTER
I wasn't. *(He looks around)* Where's Dave?

KENDRA
About that...

CARTER
I just wanna see that Boba Fett one more time.

(MAX returns with water)

MAX
Here ya go.

(CARTER downs it. He wobbles a little. KENDRA and MAX steady him)

KENDRA
We gotta get you to a hospital.

CARTER
Probably.

MAX
Do you know how to get into Dave's stuff?

CARTER
Man, I can barely remember who you are.

KENDRA
(to MAX) Al's gonna be here soon. We gotta do something.

CARTER
Al? Pacino?

(MAX thinks for a moment)

MAX
We're wasting time trying to get this thing open together. You keep working on it.

KENDRA
What're you going to do?

(MAX cocks the gun)

MAX
I'm gonna find Dave.

KENDRA
No! You can't run out on us!

CARTER
Hey, where is Dave?

MAX
He can't be too far. He didn't take his bike.

KENDRA
How do you know?

MAX
Did you hear a motorcycle fire up?

KENDRA
Oh. Right.

MAX
I know every inch of this town. I can track Dave down, and be back here before you know it.

CARTER
Is there any of that pizza left?

KENDRA
He won't come with you.

MAX
That's what the gun is for.

KENDRA
Max, please...

MAX
I'm coming back. I promise. (To CARTER) Hang in there, buddy.

CARTER
Seriously, I just want some...

(MAX runs up the stairs)

CARTER
Pizza.

(KENDRA & CARTER are silent for a bit)

CARTER
So what the hell is going on?

KENDRA
We fucked things up good, honey.

CARTER
What happened?

KENDRA
Well, I talked to Alphonse and...

CARTER
Whoa, whoa, whoa. You did what now?

KENDRA
It's the only way to get you to a hospital.

CARTER
Kendra, he is the last guy you wanna put your faith in. You know that better than anyone.

KENDRA
Look, it's done. That's not even the worst of it.

CARTER
It gets worse?

KENDRA
Dave ran off with that action figure thingy.

(Beat)

CARTER
It's worse.

KENDRA
We didn't know it when I called Alphonse! We were gonna trade it to him for getting you to a doctor.

CARTER
Wait! Shit! You didn't tell the guys...?

KENDRA
No.

CARTER
So they don't know...

KENDRA
No.

CARTER
Good. Good. *(Beat)* Yeah, this is bad.

(CARTER leans back, clearly getting weary. KENDRA goes to the safe)

CARTER
What're you doing?

KENDRA
I'm gonna try and get this thing open.

CARTER
Don't worry about it.

KENDRA
I have to, OK? I have to do something.

CARTER
That thing's like Fort Knox. So stop freaking out. Max has it covered.

KENDRA
You're putting your faith in Max? Look, he's a sweet guy, but this is...

CARTER
Kendra. Enough.

(KENDRA is silent, a little ashamed)

CARTER
I'm not mad at you, baby. But you don't get to talk about him that way anymore. He's on our side.

KENDRA
What about Dave?

CARTER
Don't worry about him.

(Beat)

CARTER
So he really ran off, huh?

KENDRA
Through the bathroom window.

CARTER
Jesus.

KENDRA
It's not fair.

CARTER
I know.

KENDRA
I mean...when does it get better for us?

CARTER
Maybe tonight.

KENDRA
I don't think so.

CARTER
Because everyone's run off? Don't worry about it.

KENDRA
Are you getting loopy again?

CARTER
No, I just...well, yeah. But I know they're gonna come back, too.

KENDRA
Probably Max. But Dave...

CARTER
Dave will be back.

KENDRA
How do you know?

CARTER
'Cause he's Luke, baby. He just went off to Degobah...but he'll be back. Luke always comes back.

KENDRA
Stay with me, honey. Don't close your eyes.

CARTER
See, that's what you don't get. It's not about special effects. It's not about...things that...it's about who you count on. Good people count on good people, and that's good, y'know?

KENDRA
Not...really?

(He touches her face, getting more   incoherent)

CARTER
You're a good person, Kendra Johnson. That means good things happen to you. But you gotta count on people to have your back.

KENDRA
I count on you.

CARTER
I know. And I count on them. That's why they're
gonna come back.

(He begins to laugh. She smiles, despite herself)

KENDRA
What is it?

CARTER
Look at me. Who am I? *(He tries to assume the pose
of Han Solo frozen in Carbonite)*

KENDRA
Don't move your arm!

CARTER
I can't even feel it anymore. Tell me who I am.

KENDRA
Oh god. There's too much blood...

CARTER
Who am I, who am I, who am I, who am I...

KENDRA
You're Carter Sloan, OK? You're a big, sweet moron
who's got to stop flailing around and...

CARTER
Nuh-uh. I'm Han Solo. And I'm frozen in Carbonite.
That means that any minute now, my buddies are
gonna come back and rescue me. And you. And the
droids. That's how it happens.

KENDRA
OK.

CARTER
And then we're gonna get married.

KENDRA

That's not what happened in the movie, sweetheart.

CARTER

Who's talking about a movie?

(She pauses for a moment)

KENDRA

You're delirious.

CARTER

Let's get married.

KENDRA

Shut up, OK? You're being crazy.

CARTER

I know. That's why you love me. So let's do it.

KENDRA

Carter, stop it.

CARTER

No. I don't stop things. I start things. And I want to
start something now. Right now. No more thinking about it. Jesus, you have no idea how long
I've been thinking about this. I wanted to find the
right way to ask you. I guess the right way is me in
your lap, bleeding all over the place. But I promise, if you say yes, I'll do it again when I'm better.
Unless you think this one is good. I kinda do.

KENDRA

You're just doing this 'cause you think we're not
gonna....

CARTER

That's not why and you know it.

(She is silent, clearly upset)

CARTER
I'm kinda woozy, so if you're gonna say yes....

KENDRA
Why?

CARTER
Why what?

KENDRA
Why me?

(Beat)

KENDRA
(Very quietly) Why me?

CARTER
Because you're a princess. You're my princess.

(KENDRA leans in and kisses him)

KENDRA
I love you.

CARTER
I know.

(MAX comes down the stairs, slowly)

CARTER
You're back! Chewie's back!

MAX
Yeah.

KENDRA
That was fast. Did you find him?

MAX
No.

KENDRA
Fuck!

MAX
You guys should...

KENDRA
I wasn't able to get Dave's thingy open either! So now we're...

MAX
Yeah, we got bigger problems right now.

(Coming down the stairs at a slowly and assured pace is ALPHONSE "THE BIG MAN" DiMARTINO. He has a box of Chinese food, and moves with the confidence of a man who is in complete control of the situation & knows it. He gets to the bottom of the stairs)

KENDRA
Alphonse.

BIG MAN
Kendra. *(He crosses to the couch and lounges across it)*

CARTER
Make yourself comfortable.

BIG MAN
Did I give you the impression that I wasn't comfortable?

MAX
Carter didn't mean any disrespect. He just...

BIG MAN
You. What's your name?

MAX
Maxwell Beauregard Farley the Third, sir.

BIG MAN
Shut up.

MAX
Yes sir.

BIG MAN
This is the crowd you hang out with now, Kendra?
Johnny Bleeds-A-Lot and this pantload?

KENDRA
They grow on you.

BIG MAN
Yeah, so do bedsores.

*(He lets them sit in uncomfortable silence as he eats
his Chinese food)*

BIG MAN
Man, this is good. You guys ever been to Imperial
Hunan? It's this little hole-in-the-wall down on
Second. It is unreal. They've got this hot and spicy
sauce they cook the shrimp in that'll blow your
mind. It makes me gassy as all hell, but it's worth
it, y'know? Am I right?

(No one says anything)

BIG MAN
That wasn't a rhetorical question, people. Am-I-
Right?

(They all ad-lib agreement)

BIG MAN
See, this is good. You're scared. That's smart. 'Cause
I gotta tell ya, this night has not gone as planned.

You people took what should've been a by-the-book operation and fucked it up beyond recognition.

KENDRA
I know that's what it looks like, but...

MAX
Carter got shot!

BIG MAN
Did you just raise your voice to me, pantload? Did you?

MAX
No sir.

BIG MAN
This should have been a good night for me. This whole thing took a lot of trust on my part, but some things are worth it. I thought you people understood that.

MAX
Well, at least...wait, can I talk now?

BIG MAN
No.

MAX
OK.

BIG MAN
Star Wars is something I take very seriously. Some people go to Church, some try to find themselves in the work, or their lovers. Me...I look at my multi-million dollar collection...and I know who I am. It's perfect. Utterly, completely perfect. Every single vehicle, action figure, souvenir piece...and every variant. I spent over five grand on a Walrus

Man who was sealed on an Obi-Wan card. Why?
Because it's the only one in existence. I have 2
people in my employ who spend 12 hours a day
online, hunting down every whisper, every rumor
about anything involving Star Wars. Am I making
myself clear? This is not a hobby for me. You people
are small timers. I am a professional. So why am I
here in some dank basement that smells a lot like
cat pee, without a single fucking collectible?!

CARTER
You've got good posture for a man with balls that
big.

BIG MAN
Excuse me?

KENDRA
Carter, honey...

CARTER
I'm just sayin', it's a pretty bold move, coming
down here by yourself. You're not armed, as far as
I can tell. I mean, I know you're trying to make
us scared of you or whatever. I guess I'm just not
seeing why we should be.

(The BIG MAN chuckles)

BIG MAN
You're right, Mr. Sloan. I'm not armed. I don't
need to be. (To KENDRA) I see why you like
him, Kendra. At first I thought it was his looks.
But he is one tough son of a bitch. I could beat
him stupid without losing a single noodle from my
Chow Mein. Besides, I've got five guys out there
who could put a bullet in each of your heads from
a hundred yards.

MAX
It's true. He does.

BIG MAN
So tell me why I'm here. I don't see my merchandise, so I'm wondering what it is you said you had that I might want.

KENDRA
We need help.

BIG MAN
Clearly.

KENDRA
Carter's been shot.

BIG MAN
He sure has.

KENDRA
We need to get him to a hospital.

BIG MAN
That's solid thinking. Right on the money. I just fail to see where I fit in.

KENDRA
We need to use your helicopter.

(Beat. The BIG MAN laughs)

BIG MAN
You have got to be kidding me.

KENDRA
We can't get to a hospital without getting arrested. We need you to fly him someplace safe.

BIG MAN
Kendra, whatever feelings I may or may not have

for you...

KENDRA
I know how this looks, but...

BIG MAN
Do not think for a second that our history gives you the kind of leeway to ask for what you're asking.

KENDRA
We can make a deal here, Alphonse. But I need you to keep a level head.

BIG MAN
You need? YOU need? Why should I give two shits what you need?

CARTER
You're here, aren't you?!

BIG MAN
To determine how badly you fucked up. Is it "break your legs" fucked up, or the other kind of fucked up?

MAX
Is that better or worse than getting our legs broke?

(BIG MAN glares at MAX, who falls silent)

KENDRA
I'm not a little girl anymore. Don't try to intimidate me. We're here to do a trade, pure and simple. And when you see what we have to offer, I think you'll be willing to negotiate.

BIG MAN
All right. I'm calm. I'm cool. I'm collected. Show me this mystery item.

(Beat)

KENDRA
I don't have it. One of my guys...is getting it.

(Beat)

BIG MAN
So you want to cut a deal with me to save your boyfriend's life, and you don't actually have anything to do business with?

KENDRA
It's on its way. I just...

BIG MAN
Jesus, you people...I swear to Christ, I can actually feel you making my blood pressure go up. And you know what? It's my own fault. I should never have gone into business with a bunch of amateurs. You people couldn't rob a fucking cookie jar!

MAX
Well, look on the bright side...

BIG MAN
Bright side? BRIGHT SIDE?!

(MAX shrinks in terror, barely able to get out the words--)

MAX
If he doesn't show up, you get to keep your two million.

BIG MAN
Keep my what?

MAX
Your money. Y'know. That you were gonna pay us. For the toys.

(The BIG MAN takes this in. Then he begins to laugh)

BIG MAN
Oh my god. I get it now...

(He laughs even harder. KENDRA & CARTER wait for the other shoe to drop. MAX, oblivious, almost joins in on the laughter)

BIG MAN
Two million...is that what you told him? Two million?

KENDRA
Wait. Hold on.

BIG MAN
You didn't tell him, did you? This poor idiot has no idea what's going on, does he?

KENDRA
Alphonse, don't.

MAX
Does he mean me? Am I the poor idiot?

CARTER
Max...

BIG MAN
You see...Max, is it?

MAX
Yes sir.

BIG MAN
Max, let me tell you a story about your good friend Carter.

CARTER
It's not what you...

BIG MAN
You. Shut up. Now. It must have been about 8 months ago. I get a phone call from Kendra. Usually, when I get a call from an ex, it's because they want to get back together or some shit like that.

KENDRA
Max, he's full of...

BIG MAN
Next time I have to tell someone to shut up, I'm ripping their tongue out of their head. Got it?

(Everyone is silent)

BIG MAN
OK. Where was I? Oh, right. Kendra. She starts telling me this sob story. Her boyfriend blew all this money on New Year's Eve, playing blackjack on some boat. How much was it again, Carter?

CARTER
You know how much.

BIG MAN
Yes, but I want to hear you say it.

(Beat)

CARTER
Fifty thousand.

MAX
What?!

KENDRA
Max, listen...

MAX
How do you lose that much money on a fucking cruise ship?!

CARTER
There was this guy from Texas...I was trashed...I
kept winning and winning and...

BIG MAN
Mr. Texan was playing your pal like a grade-A
chump.

MAX
Oh Christ...

BIG MAN
So Kendra calls me up. Says these Good Ol' Boys
are turning up the heat on Carter. It was the
whole song and dance. "They're gonna kill him,
Alphonse. They said they were gonna cut off his
nose and brand him like a steer." You should've
heard it. Now I admit. I've got a big heart.
Despite whatever happened between us in the
past, I didn't like seeing her in so much pain. So
I did the gentlemanly thing and bought up pretty
boy's debt. You see where this is going, Max?

MAX
Carter, what is he...

BIG MAN
So now Carter owes me fifty thousand...plus a
very reasonable interest. Of course he can't pay
it up front. The dink makes like 8 dollars an
hour. So he comes up with this plan. Kendra tells
him I'm a...collector of memorabilia. Now it
just so happens that Carter works at a place that
has a rather excessive amount of said memorabilia. So we cut a deal. If he can acquire for me
everything in Warehouse #6, we're square. Plain
and simple.

MAX
But...you said we were...

BIG MAN
I'm afraid my deal was with him, and only him.
There's no two million, Max. Never was. Carter
gets me my merchandise, I wipe out his debt. The
end.

(MAX goes to CARTER)

MAX
He's lying, right? You've got like a plan or something. That's what this is, right?

(Beat)

CARTER
I couldn't do it without you and Dave. I knew he
could bypass the security, and that you could get
us the truck without leaving a paper trail.

MAX
Oh my god. He's telling the truth, isn't he?

CARTER
I'm so sorry. I...

MAX
Sorry?! You're sorry!? (MAX grabs CARTER
violently, pushing KENDRA out of the way)
I'LL KILL YOU! YOU PIECE OF SHIT! HOW
COULD YOU DO THIS TO ME!!!

(CARTER cries out in pain)

MAX
Does it hurt, you son of a bitch!? Not enough!
NOT ENOUGH!

KENDRA
Max! Stop it!

MAX
That bullet should've ripped through your goddamn heart!

KENDRA
Leave him alone!

(KENDRA rushes him, and he pulls the gun on her. They struggle over the gun, but she ends up with it. She points it at his head)

BIG MAN
God, this is great.

MAX
You gonna pull the trigger, Kendra?

KENDRA
I don't want to.

MAX
Why? 'Cause I showed you a picture of my daughter? That didn't stop your boyfriend. Hell, he was there the day she was born, but I bet he didn't even blink when he sold us out.

(MAX lunges at her. They struggle. MAX ends up with the gun again. The basement door opens. DAVE enters)

DAVE
Seriously? Do you want the neighbors to call in a noise complaint?

BIG MAN
Who is that? *(To DAVE)* Who are you?

DAVE

I'm David Bullanski. This is my house. I guess that makes you my guest. Technically.

BIG MAN

Is that supposed to be funny?

(DAVE shrugs)

BIG MAN

Alright. I'm going to assume you don't know who I am...

DAVE

You're Alphonse DiMartino. Sometimes called Big Man Al. You run the bulk of the illicit activity in our fair city.

(The BIG MAN just stares at him)

DAVE

What? I watch the news. Also, I've been listening at the door.

MAX

How long?

DAVE

Long enough to hear that Carter screwed the two of us over.

CARTER

Dave...just listen to me...

DAVE

Shut up. You've forfeited your right to have an opinion. Max, give me the gun.

MAX

I don't know if that's...

(DAVE holds out his hand. MAX gives him the gun)

BIG MAN
How'd you get past my guys?

DAVE
I've lived in this house my whole life. That's how.
Now sit down.

BIG MAN
Excuse me?

DAVE
Sit down, please. We've got a lot to discuss, and I
know I'd feel better if we were all seated.

KENDRA
Dave, please. Carter's fading here.

*(DAVE takes a seat. He motions with the gun for
the others to do the same)*

DAVE
OK. Let me see if I have all the facts. You...*(Points
to CARTER)*...owe him...*(Points to the BIG
MAN)*...fifty thousand dollars.

BIG MAN
Plus interest.

DAVE
Right, of course. So you conned Max and I into
committing larceny, all on your word. That's why
we did this, Carter. Not just because you told us
we'd be filthy rich. Because you said it would be
OK.

CARTER
I'm sorry. I...

DAVE
Yes. I know. You're sorry. Sorry, sorry, sorry. It's easy to say that after you've been caught. *(Turns to the BIG MAN)* Sounds like you've got quite a collection on your hands. Any Jawas with vinyl capes?

BIG MAN
Four of them. In Boxes.

DAVE
Vlix, from the Droids cartoon?

BIG MAN
Just bought one last month. Some sucker sold it to me for 3 large.

DAVE
The Yak Face action figure, released only in Canada?

BIG MAN
Stop wasting my time.

DAVE
Bet you don't have this.

(DAVE holds up the "Holy Grail" of action figures. The BIG MAN's eyes go wide)

DAVE
This is what Kendra called you about. And yes, it is what you think it is.

BIG MAN
But...but it's impossible. It's only a myth...a legend...

DAVE
It's real. You're looking at it right now.

BIG MAN
Boba Fett...

DAVE & BIG MAN TOGETHER
With Removable Helmet.

(The BIG MAN closes in on it. DAVE raises the gun. The BIG MAN stops)

BIG MAN
Are you pointing a gun at me?

DAVE
I'm sorry. It's been a bitch of a day, so I'm afraid I have to. You can take a look at it, but I'm not letting it go.

(Beat)

BIG MAN
Fair enough.

(He removes a pair of reading glasses from his pocket)

BIG MAN
Please, could you turn it? I'd like to see the back.

(DAVE does so)

BIG MAN
My god, look at those displays. This is the Power of the Force series, isn't it?

DAVE
Yes. Take a look at the copyright.

(The BIG MAN does so)

BIG MAN
It's real. It's really real. *(He smells it)* The texture... even the smell of it...this isn't a forgery. This is genuine.

DAVE
Yes.

BIG MAN
Where...?

DAVE
There was a hidden room, in the warehouse.

(The BIG MAN takes a moment, collecting himself)

BIG MAN
I want it.

DAVE
Obviously.

BIG MAN
What's to stop me from just reaching out and taking it?

DAVE
I see one hand coming at me too fast, and I rip the package.

(The BIG MAN pauses in fear)

BIG MAN
You wouldn't.

DAVE
There are a lot of things I thought I'd never do before tonight. Now why don't we sit down like gentlemen and make a deal?

(They all sit down)

DAVE
Carter, you still with us?

(CARTER looks up, groggy)

KENDRA
Honey?

CARTER
I'm awake.

DAVE
Good. I want you to hear this. Mr. DiMartino, my
demands are simple. In exchange for this priceless
piece of nostalgia, I want the following things:
1 - You buy off the police, or whatever it is you do,
to keep us off their radar. As far as Johnny Law is
concerned, tonight's disaster never happened.
2 - Carter is taken somewhere where he can get
the appropriate medical attention.
3 - Carter's debt is wiped clean.

CARTER
Why are you...?

DAVE
Because that, Carter, is what friends do.

BIG MAN
So, those are your conditions? All of them?

DAVE
Yes. It's a good deal. You know it. I know it. Boba
Fett with Removable Helmet knows it.

(The BIG MAN considers it for a moment)

BIG MAN
Deal.

*(DAVE hands The BIG MAN the toy. The BIG
MAN pulls out a cellphone)*

BIG MAN
Hello. Dr. Dolan?

Oh, hi, Callie. Can I talk to your daddy, please?
Thanks, sweetheart.
Dolan? Yes, this Alphonse.
I need you take care of one of my people.
Tonight.
Gunshot wound. In the arm.
I know it's late. Suck it up.
He'll be there in twenty minutes.
Good.
Thank you.
(He hangs up the phone)
Kendra, get him to my car. Tell the driver to take you to Dr. Dolan's. He knows where to go.

KENDRA
Why should I trust you?

BIG MAN
Mostly 'cause you don't have a choice.

MAX
Can we just do this? He's coming apart.

(KENDRA gently tries to lift CARTER, who starts to topple. DAVE & MAX catch him)

CARTER
Max, please...I'm sorry...

MAX
I know, man. Just hold still.
CARTER
Where am I going?

KENDRA
To the doctor's, honey.

(The BIG MAN watches them struggle to move CARTER)

BIG MAN
God, look at you people. Haven't you carried a gunshot victim before?

(KENDRA pushes MAX & DAVE away, taking CARTER herself. CARTER, still very out of it, looks at the BIG MAN just before he gets carried off)

CARTER
You're not invited to the wedding.

(CARTER is led off. They look at KENDRA)

KENDRA
Yeah. That's right, bitches. We're getting married.

(MAX & KENDRA head upstairs with CARTER. Beat. BIG MAN stares at DAVE)

BIG MAN
You. What's your name again?

DAVE
Um...Dave. Dave Bullanski.

BIG MAN
You're the one who came up with the whole plan? To get into the warehouse?

DAVE
Yeah. I guess I did.

BIG MAN
You did, or you guess you did? Which is it?

DAVE
I did. Yes. I mean, Carter had the basic idea. To rob them, I mean. I just came up with a way to get past the security protocols and...

BIG MAN
Alright, alright. I don't need your life story. That
was some...hey, what's that? *(Points to the open
cabinet)*

DAVE
That's my collection.

BIG MAN
You...have a collection too?

DAVE
Yeah. It's totally awesome. I mean, it's not like
yours or anything, but...

BIG MAN
Lemme see.

(They both bask in its glory)

BIG MAN
What is it you do, Dave?

DAVE
IT for Allegiant Data Systems.

BIG MAN
You bought all these on a technician's salary?

DAVE
Yeah. It's taken years. I mean, I don't pay rent or
bills. That helps.

BIG MAN
Impressive. Most impressive. You should see mine.

DAVE
Yeah, I wish.

BIG MAN
I wasn't joking.

(DAVE stares at him, confused)

BIG MAN
You know your stuff.

DAVE
Yes. Yes, I do.

BIG MAN
How would you like to know your stuff profes-
sionally?

(Beat)

BIG MAN
I could use you on my staff. I employ a select
group who procure the rarest of memorabilia for
me. You seem extremely qualified.

(DAVE says nothing, clearly unsure)

BIG MAN
Trust me, you'll be making more than enough
money to move out of this...hole. And still have
enough left over to indulge your habit. Not many
people get paid to do what they love, Mr. Bullanski.
Make the right choice.

DAVE
Sounds a little "dark side" to me.

BIG MAN
Trust me. You're a lot closer than you think you
are.

*(The BIG MAN offers his hand. DAVE hesitates,
then shakes it. He hands DAVE a wad of bills)*

DAVE
What's this?

BIG MAN
Call it your first paycheck.

DAVE
This is a lot of money.

BIG MAN
Maybe for you.

DAVE
How do you know I'll even show up for work?
Maybe I'll just take the money and run.

*(The BIG MAN laughs, knowing full well that
DAVE wouldn't do that. He paces around the basement, taking it in)*

BIG MAN
I used to have a place just like this, when I first
got out of high school. God, that was hell. No one
understood. People like us....we're a rare breed,
Dave. We're laughed at, ridiculed...because other
people are jealous of us. They can call us dorks,
or geeks, or nerds. Makes no difference. We know
who we are. We're fans.

DAVE
Yes. Yes we are.

BIG MAN
Just look at these... *(He takes DAVE back to the
collection)* Every time I see a Star Wars collectible, still in its box...Bam! I'm a kid again. I'm
nine years old, opening up my first Tie-Fighter on
Christmas Eve. The world was a simpler place back
then. A little piece of molded plastic was able to
fire the imagination. God...they're just so damn
beautiful.

(Beat)

DAVE
You don't have a lot of friends, do you?

BIG MAN
No, Dave. I do not.

(He gives DAVE his card)

BIG MAN
Call this number on Monday. We'll send a driver
to pick you up. *(He starts to go)*

DAVE
Thank you.

*(The BIG MAN just nods, a dignified response of
respect, and walks up the stairs. DAVE closes his
cabinet, then sits down. He finds MAX's wallet
wherever KENDRA set it. He takes the BIG
MAN's money and puts it in MAX's wallet. Soon,
MAX comes running back downstairs)*

DAVE
Jesus! Keep it down.

MAX
Sorry.

*(MAX plops down on the couch next to DAVE.
DAVE grabs the box of Ding-Dongs)*

DAVE
Ding-Dong?

MAX
Sure.

(They both take a Ding-Dong and eat)

DAVE
Really think they're gonna get married?

MAX
Yup.

DAVE
Fuck.

MAX
Yup.

(Beat)

DAVE
Wanna see my collection?

(MAX shakes his head "no.")

DAVE
You sure?

(MAX nods "yes.")

DAVE
Well...what do you want to do?

MAX
I wanna go get Carrie.

DAVE
Yeah. So I'll call you tomorrow, OK?

MAX
Sure.

DAVE
We can catch a movie or something.

MAX
Sure.

(MAX starts to go. He stops, and looks at DAVE)

MAX
You saved us.

DAVE
Yeah?

MAX
Yeah.

(Beat)

MAX
See ya tomorrow. *(About to leave, then realizes he doesn't have his wallet)* Dammit. Where'd I put my wallet?

DAVE
I think it's on the dryer.

MAX
Right. *(He takes his wallet and pockets it)* So... movie? Tomorrow?

DAVE
Sure.

MAX
Can Carrie come?

DAVE
Sure.

(MAX starts to head back up the stairs)

MAX
Thanks, dude.

DAVE
No problem.

(MAX is gone. DAVE smiles)

DAVE
I've got your back.

(DAVE turns on the TV & DVD player. The theme from Star Wars plays. He leans back and gets comfortable. Lights fade)

END OF PLAY

ABOUT THE PLAYWRIGHT

Joseph Zettelmaier is a Michigan-based playwright and four-time nominee for the Steinberg/American Theatre Critics Association Award for best new play, first in 2006 for ALL CHILDISH THINGS, then in 2007 for LANGUAGE LESSONS, in 2010 for IT CAME FROM MARS and in 2012 for ALL CHILDISH THINGS. Other plays include SALVAGE, THE GRAVEDIGGER - A FRANKENSTEIN PLAY, NORTHERN AGGRESSION, DR. SEWARD'S DRACULA, INVASIVE SPECIES, THE SCULLERY MAID, NIGHT BLOOMING, and EBENEZER.

POINT OF ORIGIN won Best Locally Created Script 2002 from the Ann Arbor News, and THE STILLNESS BETWEEN BREATHS also won Best New Play 2005 from the Oakland Press. THE STILLNESS BETWEEN BREATHS and IT

CAME FROM MARS were selected to appear in the National New Play Network's Festival of New Plays. He also co-authored Flyover, USA: Voices From Men of the Midwest at the Williamston Theatre (Winner of the 2009 Thespie Award for Best New Script). He also adapted CHRISTMAS CAROL'D for the Performance Network.

IT CAME FROM MARS was a recipient of 2009's Edgerton Foundation New American Play Award, and won Best New Script 2010 from the Lansing State Journal. His play ALL CHILDISH THINGS won the Edgerton Foundation New American Play Award in 2011.

Joseph is an Associate Artist at First Folio Shakespeare, an Artistic Ambassador to the National New Play Network, and an adjunct lecturer at Eastern Michigan University, where he teaches Dramatic Composition.

More Plays From SORDELET INK

A Tale of Two Cities
by Christoper M Walsh
adapted from the novel by Charles Dickens

The Count of Monte Cristo
by Christoper M Walsh
adapted from the novel by Alexandre Dumas

The Moonstone
by Robert Kauzlaric
adapted from the novel by Wilkie Collins

Her Majesty's Will
by Robert Kauzlaric
adapted from the novel by David Blixt

Season on the Line
by Shawn Pfautsch
adapted from Herman Melville's MOBY-DICK

Hatfield & McCoy
by Shawn Pfautsch

Once A Ponzi Time
by Joe Foust

Eve of Ides
by David Blixt

VISIT WWW.SORDELETINK.COM FOR MORE!

NOVELS FROM
SORDELET INK

The Star-Cross'd Series
THE MASTER OF VERONA
VOICE OF THE FALCONER
FORTUNE'S FOOL
THE PRINCE'S DOOM
VARNISH'D FACES - STAR-CROSS'D SHORT STORIES

The Colossus Series
COLOSSUS: STONE & STEEL
COLOSSUS: THE FOUR EMPERORS
and coming 2018
COLOSSUS: WAIL OF THE FALLEN

HER MAJESTY'S WILL
a novel of Wit & Kit

All by bestselling author David Blixt!

VISIT WWW.DAVIDBLIXT.COM FOR MORE!

45641109R00095

Made in the USA
Lexington, KY
18 July 2019